T...................liction

This book is to be returned on or before
the last date stamped below

D1340178

Edited by
COLIN BREWER

Treatment Options in Addiction

Medical Management of
Alcohol and Opiate Abuse

GASKELL

Gaskell is an imprint of the Royal College of Psychiatrists,
17 Belgrave Square, London SW1

British Library Cataloguing-in-Publication Data
Treatment Options in Addiction
  I. Brewer, Colin
  616.86
  ISBN 0-902241-60-5

Distributed in North America
by American Psychiatric Press, Inc.
ISBN 0-88048-624-4

Phototypeset by Dobbie Typesetting Limited, Tavistock, Devon
Printed in Great Britain by Bell and Bain Ltd, Glasgow

Contents

Contributors

Nathan H. Azrin, Professor, Nova University, Center for Psychological Studies, 3301 College Avenue, Fort Lauderdale, Florida 33314, USA

Leonard S. Brahen, formerly Medical Director, Nassau County Department of Drug and Alcohol Addiction, and Associate Professor, State University of New York at Stonybrook – School of Medicine (currently 735 Central Ave., NY 11398, USA)

Colin Brewer, Medical Director, The Stapleford Centre, 25A Eccleston Street, London SW1W 9NP, UK

Peter Geerlings, Chairman, Department of Psychiatry, University of Amsterdam, Tafelbergweg 25, 1105 BC Amsterdam Zuidoost, The Netherlands

Kevin Gournay, Professor of Mental Health and Department Director, Health Research Centre, Middlesex University, Enfield, Middlesex EN3 4SF, UK

Nick Heather, Professor of Drug and Alcohol Studies and Director, National Drug & Alcohol Research Centre, University of New South Wales, PO Box 1 Kensington, NSW 2033, Australia

Herman Joseph, New York State Office of Alcohol and Substance Abuse Services, 55 W. 125th St, New York, NY 10027, USA

Jacques van Limbeek, Head, Epidemiologic Department of the Mental Health Section, University of Amsterdam, Tafelbergweg 25, 1105 BC Amsterdam Zuidoost, The Netherlands

Stephen Magura, National Development and Research Institutes, Inc., 11 Beach Street, New York, NY 10013, USA

John Marks, Consultant Psychiatrist, Chapel St Clinic, Widnes, Merseyside WA8 7RE, UK

Andrew Rosenblum, National Development and Research Institutes, Inc., 11 Beach Street, New York, NY 10013, USA

Preface

COLIN BREWER

In this age of information overload, the editors or authors of any new book in a field already thickly planted with competing texts need more justification than usual. Potential readers are entitled to expect it to contain information which is not just clinically useful and well referenced but also novel (or at least up to date) and not already available in an existing single text. I believe that, judged by these criteria, this book, which is based on papers presented at a symposium entitled ''Effective Treatment Options in Addiction'' held in London in 1989, can justify its existence. One reason is that many current texts reflect the traditional and still common existence of separate facilities and training for 'alcoholism' and 'drug abuse' treatment. Apart from the well documented similarities between various types of addiction (Orford, 1985), patients do not always oblige by restricting their tastes to alcohol *or* opiates (to take two of the commonest categories) but frequently abuse both.

In this highly ideological and contentious field of practice, some attempt at definition is necessary, even if it defines little more than areas of conflict. Some might feel that the use of words like 'addiction' or 'alcoholism' to cover such a wide range of conditions is vague and undesirable. It is true that terms such as 'dependence', 'abuse', 'misuse', 'excessive', 'harmful', or 'problematic' use (or in the case of illicit drugs, simply 'use') have their place, and that 'alcoholic' is regarded as an unhelpful or even pejorative label in some centres.

Nevertheless, the leading British journals in this field, which regularly include papers dealing with all of these concepts and conditions, are *Addiction* and *Alcohol & Alcoholism*. Lemere (1956) pointed out that

> ''In spite of many attempts to delineate the alcoholic personality, there remains only one characteristic which is common to all alcoholics and that is that they drink too much.''

At the turn of the century, 'morphinism' and 'cocainism' seem to have been used in much the same way. Orford (1985) refers to 'excessive appetites', and we are clearly dealing with 'excess' or 'harmfulness' in various forms. However, as generic terms, 'addiction' and 'alcoholism' are shorter than most of the alternatives and are widely used and understood in that broad sense, as well as in other, narrower senses – when so specified – as, for example, in considering pharmacological withdrawal syndromes.

There are many treatments for 'addiction', but relatively few have been shown in controlled trials to have any specific therapeutic effect. Indeed, some have never been subjected to controlled evaluation. The currently well known 'Minnesota Model' has only recently been objectively assessed and has not come out of the exercise with its colours flying (Andreasson *et al*, 1990; Keso & Salaspuro, 1990). Medical – that is, mainly pharmacological – contributions to the treatment of addiction have often been either ignored or derided, especially by the many people working in the field who are not medically qualified. It is therefore particularly fitting that Chapter 1 should be by Professor Nick Heather, a psychologist. He concludes that the evidence for a high level of effectiveness of disulfiram treatment is strong. However, it must be administered under supervision rather than just by giving the patient a bottle of tablets and hoping that he will take them regularly.

Heather not only identifies demonstrably ineffective treatments for alcohol abuse, but also notes the paradox that several of them feature prominently in standard treatment programmes – both private and publicly funded – in many countries, while the most effective treatments often do not feature at all, even though most are also cost-effective. Indeed, the symposium had its origins in a feeling that addiction treatment is not merely influenced but characterised by a concentration on techniques which have been shown, often repeatedly, in controlled studies, to be ineffective. As Gunne (1990) has noted, there are too many ''enthusiastic amateurs'', who often have ''a hostile attitude to the medical profession and after a while also to evaluation research based on hard – and sometimes unpleasant – facts''. To concentrate on effectiveness needs little defence, but in recessional times cost-effectiveness is especially important, and most treatments which have been shown to make a significant impact are relatively cheap.

The evidence for the effectiveness of supervised disulfiram comes from a number of studies by different teams at different centres, all reaching the same conclusion. The most convincing, however, are those carried out by Azrin and his colleagues, starting with research published as long ago as 1973. Professor Azrin describes, in Chapter 2, how, as a behavioural psychologist, he had hoped to show the effectiveness of carefully designed and targeted behavioural programmes in alcoholism, but found to his surprise that for many patients, merely ensuring adequate supervision of disulfiram gave results which were equally good, whether or not these subjects also received intensive behavioural and social support.

Although the research carried out by Azrin and his colleagues, and their excellent therapeutic results, are quite often cited, the contribution of disulfiram is usually overlooked, and he had not previously been invited to speak on the subject in the UK. The review of a representative selection of current British and US alcoholism treatment textbooks, which follows Azrin's chapter, reveals the surprising fact that most of them do not discuss either his use of disulfiram or the specific comments in papers both by himself and other researchers about the importance (and cost-effectiveness) of adequate supervision. In Chapter 4, I review the use of disulfiram in the probation and criminal justice setting, and discuss some of the clinical aspects of disulfiram treatment. I have incorporated some important research into the pharmacokinetics, mode of action, toxicity, bioavailability, and dosage of disulfiram which has been published since the symposium was held.

Naltrexone is a relatively new drug in the UK, having become available only in 1985, and receiving its full product licence in 1988. However, it has been used in the US since the early 1970s, and few people can have had more experience of it in various settings than Dr Leonard Brahen of New York. His conclusions about its safety are particularly reassuring. A recent study (Pini *et al*, 1991) confirms previous reports of the lack of any significant hepatotoxicity. I then describe my experience with naltrexone in British opiate addicts, with special reference to the way in which it can considerably speed up the withdrawal process, when combined with other drugs. As with disulfiram, the importance of consistent supervised administration in preventing relapse is emphasised.

Although this volume concentrates particularly on pharmacological treatments, neither the contributors nor editor intend to suggest that psychological or social aspects of treatment are unimportant. However, Azrin's chapter makes the important practical and economic point that many patients do not need intensive psychotherapy or counselling, as opposed to support and encouragement. There are, of course, many textbooks on counselling and psychotherapy, both in general and as applied specifically to addictive behaviour.

The symposium's emphasis on effectiveness implied a preference for psychological interventions which make a demonstrable and specific impact, over those which are essentially a variety of placebo activity. Dr Kevin Gournay, with a background in psychiatric nursing and behaviour therapy, expands on some of the points made by Heather and Azrin. He discusses the prevalence and relevance of certain common underlying psychological problems, notably phobic anxiety, and the most effective psychological techniques to employ against them. Here, the evidence strongly favours behavioural as opposed to psychodynamic methods. A similar conclusion about the effectiveness of various social work techniques has recently been reached by Macdonald *et al* (1992). Gournay emphasises the crucial importance of learning to cope with anxiety by exposure to feared situations in realistic settings, and explains how drugs like disulfiram and naltrexone can facilitate this process.

Two controlled studies, published since the symposium, have confirmed the effectiveness of methadone maintenance in cultures as varied as Sweden and Thailand (Gunne, 1990; Vanichseni *et al*, 1991). They also demonstrate that the *average* daily dosage needs to be nearer 100 mg than the 50–60 mg which is commonly the *maximum* permitted dosage in many programmes.

What is less well known about the Swedish study is that after the results became known, the authorities decided to close down the methadone programme on the grounds that it offered unfair competition to drug-free treatment. This argument was abandoned when some of the patients in the methadone programme, on learning that their principal lifeline was about to be severed, threatened action against the Minister concerned, who eventually conceded defeat.

Nevertheless, methadone treatment has had a very mixed press since its introduction in the early 1960s and has gone through several cycles of popularity and disapproval. In the age of acquired immune deficiency syndrome (AIDS), objections seem to be diminishing, but they are still strong in some quarters, and several parts of the UK seem almost proud of being virtually methadone-free. After a brief review by Brahen of the pharmacology of both methadone and its longer-acting analogue laevo-alpha-acetyl methadol (LAAM), Dr John Marks delivers a radical critique of the whole prohibitionist philosophy, coming down in favour of a middle way between unlimited availability and heavy policing. Dr Peter Geerlings of Amsterdam then describes how the relatively relaxed Dutch attitude to making methadone available works in practice. Following in this liberal tradition, Derks (1990*a,b*) has recently published the results of an experiment in Amsterdam with the prescribing of intravenous morphine, which is an important contribution to the debate about a particularly controversial area of opiate maintenance treatment.

Both alcohol and opiate abuse are factors in a sizeable proportion of criminal activity, and those actually charged with alcohol- and heroin-related offences contribute significantly to the workload of courts and prisons. Part of the symposium was devoted to ways in which the very high relapse rate in this group can be reduced, and to alternatives to incarceration, especially now that AIDS casts a large and frightening shadow on most prison services. Dr Stephen Magura presents a description of the history and operation of the methadone programme in one of the New York jails. Dr Brahen's encouraging experience with naltrexone in the criminal justice system has already been mentioned and as with disulfiram, the period following the symposium has seen the publication of some important studies of naltrexone. They confirm the significant effectiveness of naltrexone in controlling offending behaviour, compared with ordinary probation management, when its administration is properly supervised.

The path of therapeutic progress is littered with the wreckage of good ideas that did not work in practice. However, the ability to detect and quantify both prescribed and unprescribed drugs in hair (as opposed to urine) seems likely to simplify enormously both the monitoring of compliance with treatment and the detection of relapses. This technique is reviewed in Chapter 12. If it also enables researchers to improve their assessments of the effectiveness of treatment, it may assist therapeutic progress generally as well as helping individual patients.

This collection of papers is not presented as a comprehensive guide to all the effective methods (let alone the numerous ineffective ones) of managing alcohol and opiate abuse. Notably absent are papers about the treatment of severe alcohol withdrawal or about conventional in-patient opiate withdrawal programmes. That is because there is relatively little disagreement in these areas of practice and they are generally well documented. This book has deliberately concentrated on a selection of techniques which are commonly ignored, sketchily described, misrepresented, or poorly referenced in many existing texts.

There are other promising techniques being developed, such as long-acting injections of naltrexone and disulfiram which will both remove the need for frequent oral administration and reduce the risk of evasion (Phillips & Greenberg, 1992). Existing depot preparations of disulfiram have no useful pharmacological effects, but they may have a useful placebo effect in some patients (Johnsen & Morland, 1992).

Two recent studies (Volpicelli *et al*, 1992; O'Malley *et al*, 1992) show that in addition to its use as a relapse-prevention agent in opiate dependence, naltrexone can significantly reduce both craving and alcohol consumption in patients having treatment for alcohol dependence but who are not opiate abusers. In both reports, the authors speculate about possible links between opioid receptors, endorphins and alcohol abuse. The trials were based on animal studies which indicate that morphine tends to increase alcohol consumption while opiate antagonists tend to decrease it. Further confirmation of these interesting findings may generate some new, useful and testable hypotheses about the biology of alcohol abuse.

Possible blocking agents for other drugs of abuse such as cocaine, tranquillisers, and even nicotine are being studied. Implanted devices sensitive to the use of alcohol and other drugs could release a blocking agent if a particular drug were used. The important problem of how to detect intermittent alcohol use or abuse in patients who are supposed to be abstaining may be simplified by the development of skin patches or electronic devices which can monitor the concentration of alcohol in sweat (Phillips, 1984). Such devices would have to incorporate methods for detecting tampering.

Any psychiatrist or psychologist contemplating a shelf of largely unused long-playing records as he listens to his compact disc player has cause to reflect on the fact that progress in technology is more rapid than progress in psychotherapy or psychopharmacology. Science and technology have brought developments in medicine and surgery that were undreamed of even ten years ago. So far, they have hardly had a chance to show what they can do for drug and alcohol abuse.

References

ANDREASSON, S., PARMANDER, M. & ALLEBECK, P. (1990) A trial that failed and the reasons why: comparing the Minnesota Model with out-patient treatment and non-treatment of alcohol disorders. *Scandinavian Journal of Social Medicine*, **18**, 221–224.

DERKS, J. (1990a) The efficacy of the Amsterdam morphine-dispensing programme. In *Drug Misuse & Dependence* (eds H. Ghodse, C. Kaplan & R. Mann). Carnforth: Parthenon.

—— (1990b) The Amsterdam morphine-dispensing experiment. *International Journal of Medicine & Law*, **9**, 841–853.

GUNNE, L. (1990) Politicians and scientists in the combat against drug abuse. *Drug & Alcohol Dependence*, **25**, 241–244.

JOHNSEN, J. & MORLAND, J. (1992) Depot preparations of disulfiram: experimental and clinical results. *Acta Psychiatrica Scandinavica*, **86**, 27–30.

KESO, L. & SALASPURO, M. (1990) In-patient treatment of employed alcoholics: a randomised clinical trial of Hazelden-type and traditional treatments. *Alcoholism: Clinical & Experimental Research*, **14**, 584–589.

LEMERE, F. (1956) The nature and significance of brain damage from alcoholism. *American Journal of Psychiatry*, **113**, 361–362.

MACDONALD, G., SHELDON, B. & GILLESPIE, J. (1992) Contemporary studies of the effectiveness of social work. *British Journal of Social Work*, **22**, 615–643.

O'MALLEY, S. S., JAFFE, A. J., CHANG, G., *et al* (1992) Naltrexone and coping skills therapy for alcohol dependence: a controlled study. *Archives of General Psychiatry*, **49**, 881–887.

ORFORD, J. (1985) *Excessive Appetites*. Oxford: Oxford University Press.

PHILLIPS, M. (1984) Sweat-patch testing detects inaccurate self-reports of alcohol consumption. *Alcoholism: Clinical & Experimental Research*, **8**, 51–53.

—— & GREENBERG, J. (1992) Dose-ranging study of depot disulfiram in alcohol abusers. *Alcoholism: Clinical & Experimental Research*, **16**, 964–967.

PINI, L., FERRETTI, C., TRENTI, T., *et al* (1991) Effects of long-term treatment with naltrexone on hepatic enzyme activity. *Drug Metabolism & Drug Interactions*, **9**, 161–174.

VANICHSENI, S., WONGSUWAN, B., THE STAFF OF BMA NARCOTICS CLINIC NO. 6., *et al* (1991) A controlled trial of methadone maintenance in a population of intravenous drug users in Bangkok: implications for prevention of HIV. *International Journal of Addictions*, **26**, 1313–1320.

VOLPICELLI, J. R., ALTERMAN, A. I., HAYASHIDA, M., *et al* (1992) Naltrexone in the treatment of alcohol dependence. *Archives of General Psychiatry*, **49**, 876–880.

1 Disulfiram treatment for alcohol problems: is it effective and, if so, why?

NICK HEATHER

Since it was accidentally discovered in Denmark in 1948, there have been literally hundreds of reports and discussion papers in the literature about the effectiveness of oral disulfiram. Many of these have simply followed up patients treated with disulfiram and have come to favourable conclusions, with success rates ranging from 19% to 89% (Miller & Hester, 1980). Unfortunately, much the same could probably be said of virtually any treatment approach to alcohol problems, and uncontrolled studies of this kind do not help us to arrive at scientifically reliable conclusions regarding effectiveness.

Several studies have reported that patients who voluntarily accept disulfiram do better than those who refuse it (e.g. Wexberg, 1953; Hoff, 1961) and two large outcome studies (Gerard & Saenger, 1966; Armor *et al*, 1978) have found that disulfiram is associated with favourable outcome among large samples of treated problem drinkers. But the problems of interpretation here are obvious; patients who accept disulfiram may be better motivated to succeed with any type of treatment.

There is also evidence in the older literature (see Baekeland *et al*, 1971) that, among those taking disulfiram, patients who comply better (i.e. take their disulfiram regularly) have a better outcome than those who comply less well. Interestingly, the same factors (older, fewer psychological complications, more severe alcohol problems) predict both better compliance and better outcome (Baekeland *et al*, 1971). However, these factors are probably not specific to disulfiram treatment.

Controlled trials of unsupervised disulfiram

According to Fuller *et al* (1986) the drug is normally used in clinical practice "in combination with alcoholism counselling and given to patients to take at home". There may, in fact, be some dispute about how normal this use of unsupervised disulfiram is, especially in Europe (Brewer, 1987), but it is undoubtedly the form which has received the most attention in controlled trials of the drug's effectiveness.

As this implies, there have been several controlled trials of disulfiram administered in roughly this fashion, with the earliest of these studies (Wallerstein *et al*, 1957) producing the most encouraging results. However, all earlier studies suffer from considerable problems with experimental design, including non-random assignment, non-blind assessment, large follow-up attrition, reliance on patients' self-reports of drinking, small sample sizes, short follow-up, and failure to specify outcomes in objective terms (see Miller & Hester, 1980). Thus, it will be more profitable to concentrate on two more recent controlled trials carried out at the same research centre, which are some of the best-designed and implemented studies, not merely in the area of disulfiram, but in the alcoholism field generally. We may therefore regard their results with reasonable confidence.

Fuller & Roth (1979) studied 128 male alcoholics at a Veterans Administration Hospital who were willing to take disulfiram. Patients were excluded from the trial if they were not living with relatives, were 60 years or older, or showed medical contraindications for disulfiram; 61% of subjects were black. All patients had counselling for their alcohol problems, as well as disulfiram treatment. Subjects were randomly allocated to the following three groups:

(1) instructed to take a standard-dose regime of disulfiram (500 mg daily for one week and 250 mg daily thereafter)
(2) instructed to take daily capsules containing a pharmacologically inactive dose of disulfiram (1 mg)
(3) instructed to take one 50 mg riboflavin tablet daily.

Patients in groups 1 and 2 were blind as to which level of disulfiram they were taking. Group 2 was included as a control for the threat of the disulfiram–ethanol reaction (DER) and group 3 was a control for the care and attention that all patients received.

Other important design features were that both treaters and assessors were blind to treatment group and that a riboflavin marker was used in all groups as a measure of compliance with the regime. Intake of disulfiram was monitored throughout the year of the study. Follow-up was carried out frequently for up to one year by both a doctor and a social worker independently. Confirmation of self-reports of alcohol consumption was obtained by liver-function tests and collateral interviews; 126 out of 128 subjects completed the final assessment.

The main results of this impressively thorough study were given in percentages of complete abstinence for each group at follow-up. These were: group 1 = 21%; group 2 = 25%; group 3 = 12%. Despite the apparent superiority of groups 1 and 2, however, there was no significant difference in abstinence rate between groups 1 and 2 combined and group 3, although the authors warn that this result entails a high probability of type II error (i.e. of accepting the null hypothesis of no difference between groups when it is in fact false). There were also no significant differences between groups in drinking days, working days, family stability, percentage of scheduled appointments kept, or compliance with medication. On the basis of these results, the authors concluded that "disulfiram is of limited effectiveness in treating alcoholic patients from a population similar to the one we studied" (p. 903).

In a subsequent paper, Fuller & Williford (1980) analysed the same data by life-table methods – a statistical technique developed to analyse longitudinal data such as the response to treatment over time. On this occasion, they found that the abstinence rate for groups 1 and 2 combined (see above) was statistically superior to that for the control subjects in group 3. This suggests that unsupervised disulfiram is effective in delaying relapse and, further, that the mechanism of this effectiveness is the threat of the DER rather than any pharmacological effect of disulfiram itself.

Fuller *et al* (1986) used essentially the same design and methods in a multicentre study involving 605 male alcoholics. On this occasion, the authors found no significant differences between groups in total abstinence, time to first drink, employment, or social stability. Total abstinence rates were: group 1 = 18.8%; group 2 = 22.5%; group 3 = 16.1%. However, among those patients who had drunk during the one-year follow-up period and who had complete follow-up records, those in group 1 reported significantly fewer drinking days than patients in the control groups. These patients who had reduced frequency of drinking tended to be older and more socially stable. It is a pity that these authors did not measure quantity of alcohol consumption or extent of alcohol-related problems.

Fuller *et al*'s conclusion from their results was that "disulfiram may help to reduce drinking frequency after relapse, but does not enhance counselling in aiding alcoholic patients to sustain continuous abstinence or delay the resumption of drinking" (p. 1449). They note that Fuller & Williford (1980) had obtained a different result with respect to time to relapse but point out that the later study involved a much larger sample and multidisciplinary treatment staff, rather than the single therapist of the earlier study. However, this does not seem sufficient reason for rejecting the finding of the earlier study; it may be that the lower degree of experimental control involved in a large multicentre trial, as well as variations in the skill and commitment among the therapists taking part, diluted the impact of a treatment effect which the earlier and more rigorously controlled study had detected. It may also be possible that differences in the populations sampled, especially the preponderance of black patients in the earlier study, were responsible for the difference in results.

Moreover, the fact that disulfiram reduced the frequency of drinking among a segment of the treatment sample is a not inconsiderable achievement.

It is only by assuming that total abstinence is the sole aim of treatment that it becomes unimportant. But Chick *et al* (1988) found, in a comparison of treatment and simple advice to patients, that treatment did not increase abstinence, but only reduced the degree of alcohol-related damage in the two years before follow-up. This provided empirical support for the main conclusion of Emrick's (1975) earlier and much-quoted review of alcoholism treatment. Thus, from the increasingly influential 'harm reduction' view of treatment for alcohol problems, a reduction in the frequency of drinking might be, depending on the degree of associated harm, a clinically important effect of disulfiram.

Ways of increasing compliance

Another of Fuller *et al*'s (1986) conclusions from their study was:

> "The effectiveness of disulfiram . . . in promoting abstinence was limited because the majority of patients did not take disulfiram regularly." (p. 1454)

This makes clear that the negative results of the study should be seen as applying only to the use of 'unsupervised' disulfiram, in the manner of administration the authors regard as normal. However, the conclusion that the chief problem in disulfiram treatment was one of patient compliance appears to have been reached by many workers in the field much earlier, in the early 1970s. Indeed, at about that time, efforts commenced to discover practical ways to increase the patient's compliance with taking disulfiram, and several of these will now be discussed.

Disulfiram implants

The most obvious method is by implanting a long-acting dose of disulfiram. This was pioneered by Wilson (1975) in Canada, who made a small incision in the lower abdomen and inserted a number of disulfiram tablets below the skin within subcutaneous fat before suturing the incision. Uncontrolled studies of this method have reported favourable results (see Miller & Hester, 1980) and a randomised, controlled study by Wilson *et al* (1976) found a superior outcome among skid-row alcoholics given disulfiram implants than those given placebo. However, the only outcome measure used was time to first drink, and reports of abstinence were based only on patients' self-reports. Later work has failed to detect any pharmacological activity from disulfiram only a few weeks after implantation (Bergstrom *et al*, 1982; Morland *et al*, 1984). A lack of clinical effect of disulfiram implants in comparison with placebo has also been reported by Johnsen *et al* (1987) from Norway. Evidence of this kind has led to a general loss of interest in implanted disulfiram in treatment.

Increasing the frequency of out-patient visits

Gerrein *et al* (1973) randomly assigned 49 out-patient alcoholics, who had accepted disulfiram, to one of four treatment conditions:

(1) given disulfiram once a week
(2) given disulfiram twice weekly under supervision
(3) not given disulfiram, attending once a week
(4) not given disulfiram, attending twice weekly.

Patients in group 1 were given a seven-day supply of disulfiram (250 mg) by a doctor, and were told to take one tablet a day and return once a week for further medication. Patients in group 2 took one 250 mg tablet in the presence of a staff member and were given enough tablets for once-daily self-administration until the next clinic evening, three or four days later. All groups received a similar amount of counselling.

The results of this study are shown in Table 1.1. It will be seen that patients in group 2 had a higher abstinence rate than those in the other groups at eight-week follow-up but, unfortunately, the authors provide no information on the statistical significance of this difference. There was also a higher proportion of patients remaining in treatment in group 2 than in the other three groups. Although this study was limited to a short follow-up and a small study sample, the results do provide *prima facie* evidence of the superiority of giving disulfiram twice weekly under supervision. It should be noted that, even if patients in group 2 did not take disulfiram at home, the typical duration of disulfiram's pharmacological effect (two or three days) meant that a DER would almost certainly occur if ever the patient drank. This was not the case with patients in group 1. However, we cannot be sure that it was the frequency of visits which was responsible for the apparent superiority of results in group 2, since the issue of frequency is confounded in the design with that of supervision of the administration. It may be that supervised administration by itself was the effective ingredient.

Using disulfiram as a contingency for reinforcement

This method of increasing compliance consists of making the provision of some event that is known to be reinforcing to a client contingent on

TABLE 1.1
Percentage of patients still abstinent at eight-week follow-up

	Once-weekly visit	Twice-weekly visits (under supervision)
Given disulfiram	7%	40%
Not given disulfiram	3%	9%

Adapted from Gerrein *et al* (1973).

the taking of disulfiram. The general method is, of course, based on the principles of operant conditioning. An example will make the method clearer.

Liebson & Bigelow (1972) presented a case report in which a 'dually addicted' patient (i.e. one showing evidence of severe dependence on both heroin and alcohol) was given his daily dose of methadone only if he had ingested a suspension of disulfiram under a nurse's observation. Preliminary results of this technique were promising. Subsequent communications from this group (e.g. Liebson *et al*, 1973) have confirmed this promise. Liebson *et al* (1978) studied 25 male, alcoholic, methadone patients who were rejects from traditional treatment programmes. Patients in the treatment group were made subject to the contingencies described above, and were compared with control patients who were urged to take disulfiram but given methadone regardless of whether they took it or not. During a six-month treatment period, the results showed a highly significant difference in frequency of drinking in favour of the treatment group and non-significant trends towards better arrest rate, employment status, and drug use. Again, the study sample was small, but the results clearly suggest a highly effective method of increasing compliance among recalcitrant individuals from this particular population.

In another application of the same principles by the Johns Hopkins group, Bigelow *et al* (1976) used a security-deposit contingency contracting procedure among out-patient alcoholics. Patients agreed to deposit a sum of money, usually between US$100 and US$150, to serve as an incentive for continuing to take disulfiram on schedule (once a day for 14 days and alternate days thereafter). Failure to report to the clinic to take disulfiram under a nurse's observation resulted in a portion of the security deposit being sent to a nominated charity, the balance being returned to the patient at the end of the agreed contract (a minimum of three months). Results were promising, with 80% of 20 patients showing longer periods of abstinence immediately following entry into the programme than at any time during the previous three years. Thus, using patients as their own controls, the method was shown to be an effective way of increasing abstinence.

The contingency investigated by Haynes (1973) was the reinstatement of a jail sentence among chronic 'revolving door' alcoholics with frequent arrests for public intoxication, who had chosen one year's probation with disulfiram treatment in preference to a jail sentence. Failure to visit a probation officer twice a week to take disulfiram under supervision meant immediate arrest and reinstatement of the suspended sentence. At the end of one year, 66 out of 138 individuals were still taking disulfiram and the arrest rate for the entire cohort had dropped from 3.8 per individual in the year before the programme to 0.3 in the year of the programme. Once more, on the basis of inference drawn from using subjects as their own controls, this was a highly successful programme among a notoriously difficult population of alcoholics. Using a similar procedure, Brewer & Smith (1983) reported that nine out of 16 habitual drunkenness offenders were entirely successful while under court supervision.

Finally in this section, Sereny *et al* (1986) studied a group of patients who wished to remain connected to a treatment clinic but who had drunk repeatedly during treatment. The authors introduced a programme of mandatory, supervised disulfiram for such patients, with the coercion that failure to report to the clinic three times a week to take disulfiram would result in the termination of clinic services. Of 68 patients who agreed to this regime, 60% achieved significant periods of sobriety, with a probability of abstinence considerably higher than the average for past admissions to the clinic. The authors suggest that a controlled trial of their method is needed.

Developments in detecting disulfiram compliance

Clearly, any method aimed at increasing compliance with taking disulfiram would be greatly assisted by improvements in techniques designed to monitor such compliance by laboratory tests. There has been some attention paid to this topic in recent years.

We noted earlier that Fuller *et al* (1983), in their controlled trials of unsupervised disulfiram, used a riboflavin marker to examine compliance; they presented data from urine analysed for riboflavin during one-year follow-up. They found that excellent attendance at the clinic, submission of a large number of positive urine samples, and a period of continuous compliance with the disulfiram regime were highly associated with infrequent drinking. Fuller & Neiderhiser (1981) described an alternative method of monitoring compliance – testing for the excretion of a urinary metabolite of disulfiram, diethylamine – and report results of a longitudinal study over one year.

The use of urinary diethylamine as a marker was also described by Gordis & Peterson (1977). They found that, of 95 patients who said they were taking disulfiram, only 80% had diethylamine in their urine. The main alternative to urinary diethylamine is exhaled carbon disulphide, which was first described by Paulson *et al* (1977). These authors found that 35% of patients claiming to be taking their disulfiram were not and that, of patients whom the nurse administering the medication believed to be complying, 20% were not doing so. These results, together with those of Gordis & Peterson (1977), emphasise the unreliability of patients' self-reports in this area. More recently, Rychtarik *et al* (1983) reported on an abbreviated form of the carbon disulphide test, taking one rather than six minutes.

The potential usefulness of these technical improvements was demonstrated by Kofoed (1987) who, in a controlled comparison, showed that making available the results of a biochemical monitoring procedure (carbon disulphide) increased disulfiram compliance, compared with conditions where compliance was not monitored and where it was monitored but the results not made available.

Supervised administration

Much of the foregoing discussion of ways of increasing compliance has centred round the notion of supervised administration of disulfiram. For example, the provision of reinforcers contingent upon taking disulfiram, discussed above, obviously requires some kind of supervised administration in order to work. However, there is also the question of whether supervised administration on its own, without consequences necessarily following from it, is an effective procedure.

The first examination of supervised administration was reported over 25 years ago by Bourne *et al* (1966). They looked at the effects of supervision by patients' relatives or probation officers on skid-row alcoholics ordered by the courts to take disulfiram daily on suspended sentences. There was also a group of alcoholic volunteers, not instructed by the courts, who took their medication under the supervision of relatives only. After a demonstration of the correct method of administration in the doctor's office, the relative was asked to take responsibility for ensuring that the prescribed tablet was properly taken each morning and to contact the doctor if for any reason the patient stopped taking the medication. Although this was not a controlled trial, the results were impressive, with 32 of the 64 volunteers and 61 of the 132 compulsory patients still abstinent at nine months' follow-up. Many of the successes were individuals who had shown repeated failures in previous treatment.

An interesting approach to supervised disulfiram was taken by Robichaud *et al* (1979), who monitored the absenteeism rates of industrial employees referred by their employers for alcoholism treatment. This was done during a pre-treatment phase, during treatment by routine, supervised disulfiram administration, and again post-treatment. Disulfiram was supervised by a nurse daily for the first 14 days and on alternate days thereafter. The median percentage of absent work days was: pre-treatment $= 9.8\%$, treatment $= 1.7\%$, post-treatment $= 6.7\%$. The rate of absenteeism in the treatment phase was significantly less than during the other phases, and represented a fivefold reduction in absenteeism. Thus, while it was in effect, the supervised disulfiram regime appeared highly efficacious in reducing alcohol-related absenteeism in this industrial context.

The contracting approach

In a sense, all arrangements for taking disulfiram under supervision constitute an informal or implicit contract, but in the approach to be discussed in this section, this contract is made explicit, by clearly stipulating mutual obligations between patients and those who are to supervise their medication. In particular, contracts between marriage partners have been the focus of much of the research in question.

Marital contracts containing reference to the taking of disulfiram are an important part of the behavioural marital therapy approach developed by O'Farrell *et al* (1985). Although the separate contribution of disulfiram to this method has not been evaluated, O'Farrell & Bayog (1986) discuss the role of disulfiram contracts in treatment. The procedure they recommend is designed both to maintain disulfiram ingestion and abstinence from alcohol by the patient, and to reduce the frequency of alcohol-related arguments and quarrels between the alcoholic and spouse. The alcoholic agrees to take disulfiram each day while the spouse observes, and the spouse, in turn, agrees to record the observation of the taking of disulfiram on a calendar provided by the therapist. Both partners agree to refrain from discussions about the alcoholic's past or possible future drinking. The authors present two cases illustrating the successful use of the procedure.

Keane *et al* (1984) compared a home-based contracting programme with a control condition involving no contract or recording of disulfiram administration. With patients just about to be discharged from in-patient treatment, a meeting was arranged between the patient, a significant other, and the therapist. It was agreed that both parties to the contract would sign and post forms to the clinic each week, stating that disulfiram had been properly ingested. There was some evidence that the contracting/recording group was superior to the control group in terms of disulfiram compliance.

Undoubtedly the most successful use of disulfiram contracting in the literature is that reported by Azrin and his colleagues. Azrin (1976) described improvements to the highly effective community reinforcement approach (CRA) previously evaluated by Hunt & Azrin (1973). The improvements consisted mainly of the incorporation of a 'buddy system' to provide each client with a peer-adviser, a daily report procedure, group counselling, and a special 'social motivation programme' designed to increase self-administration of disulfiram. In the last-named, clients were first taught to view disulfiram usage in a positive manner and were asked to nominate someone, usually a spouse, to supervise daily administration. Other procedures were effected in the attempt to make the taking of disulfiram a firmly established habit.

The results of the study showed that at two-year follow-up the nine men in the improved CRA drank less, worked more, and spent more time at home and less time in institutions than nine matched controls who were given standard hospital treatment including disulfiram in the usual, unsupervised manner. The results from the CRA group are some of the most successful outcomes ever reported for treatment of alcohol problems, but may be regarded as reflecting the time, effort, and money that was put into treatment. If anything, however, the use of disulfiram made this treatment approach more economical.

The specific role of disulfiram in the success of the CRA was investigated by Azrin *et al* (1982). They randomly allocated 43 out-patient alcoholics to:

TABLE 1.2
Mean number of days of abstinence during the 30 days before interview for single and married clients

	Single	Married
Traditional disulfiram	6.75	17.4
Supervised disulfiram	8.0	30.0
Supervised disulfiram + CRA	28.3	30.0

Adapted from Azrin *et al* (1982, p. 110).

(1) traditional disulfiram treatment without supervision
(2) a socially motivated disulfiram assurance programme, similar to that described above
(3) the disulfiram assurance programme combined with community reinforcement.

Overall, the results at six-month follow-up showed that, on a range of measures, group 3 was significantly superior to group 2, which was significantly superior to group 1. Thus, supervised disulfiram administration was better than traditional, unsupervised administration, and behaviour therapy added to disulfiram was more effective than disulfiram alone.

However, there was an important interaction in the data between drinking outcome and marital status of the client which is shown in Table 1.2. For single clients, supervised disulfiram alone was ineffective, but the addition of behaviour therapy, in the form of the CRA, led to a substantial increase in effectiveness of treatment. On the other hand, for married clients, there was no additional benefit from behaviour therapy, since abstinent days had already reached a ceiling with supervised disulfiram alone. This makes sense if one assumes that the social support of a partner is necessary for successful supervised administration to take place and that married clients already had access to many of the material and social reinforcers provided by the CRA.

The results of Azrin *et al* provide the only direct comparison of supervised and unsupervised disulfiram in the literature, with conclusions very much in favour of the former. The only criticisms that can be made of this study are that there is no mention of blind follow-up, that follow-up was restricted to six months and that the sample size per group was relatively small (see Liskow & Goodwin, 1987). However, the last point is relevant only to the external validity of the conclusions (i.e. their generalisability to other samples of alcoholics) and not to their internal validity (i.e. the confidence we may have that they represent valid inferences from this particular study).

Is disulfiram effective?

It is now time to answer the main question with which this chapter is concerned. In a review of the effectiveness of treatment for alcohol problems,

TABLE 1.3
Supported versus standard alcoholism treatment methods

Treatment methods currently supported by controlled outcome methods	Treatment methods currently employed as standard practice in alcoholism programmes
Aversion therapies	Alcoholics Anonymous
Behavioural self-control training	Alcoholism education
Community reinforcement approach	Confrontation
Marital and family therapy	Group therapy
Social-skills training	Individual counselling
Stress management	Disulfiram

Adapted from Miller & Hester (1986).

Miller & Hester (1986) concluded with a short-list of treatment methods that were supported by controlled outcome research, and compared this with a further list of treatment methods which were standard practice in alcoholism programmes in the USA. The two lists are shown in Table 1.3. The point is that there is no overlap between the two lists; those methods for which research support exists are not commonly in use and those that are commonly in use are not supported by outcome research. It will be noted that disulfiram is placed in the list of commonly used methods for which no support exists.

In view of the evidence that has been reviewed in this chapter, it is appropriate to revise Miller & Hester's conclusions along the lines of Table 1.4. First, a distinction is introduced between 'supervised' and 'unsupervised' disulfiram since the research reviewed clearly shows that such a distinction is warranted in practice. Perhaps 'supervised' disulfiram should be regarded as a short-hand way of referring to the use of disulfiram accompanied by some proven method of increasing compliance, since that is the crucial point about the distinction between the two forms of use.

As we have seen, there is some evidence from the work of the Fuller group to suggest that unsupervised disulfiram is an effective treatment for alcohol problems, despite the authors' own negative conclusions from their research. However, in view of the difference in results between Fuller & Williford (1980) and Fuller *et al* (1986), the position with regard to abstinent outcomes

TABLE 1.4
Supported versus standard alcoholism treatment methods (revised version)

Treatment methods currently supported by controlled outcome methods	Treatment methods currently employed as standard practice in alcoholism programmes
Aversion therapies	Alcoholics Anonymous
Behavioural self-control training	Alcoholism education
Community reinforcement approach	Confrontation
Marital and family therapy	Group therapy
Social-skills training	Individual counselling
Stress management	Disulfiram without supervision
Disulfiram with supervision	

is unclear. The evidence that unsupervised disulfiram is effective in reducing frequency of drinking among a segment of the treatment population was not based on a comparison of randomly assigned groups and, to that extent, is tentative. If it eventually transpires that disulfiram given in the traditional manner is an effective treatment, the size of this effect is unlikely to be large. Thus, unsupervised disulfiram remains for the present on the right-hand side of Table 1.4.

The justification for placing supervised disulfiram on the left-hand side of Table 1.4 comes mainly from the work of Azrin *et al* (1982). Here, it was clearly shown that supervised disulfiram is superior to unsupervised disulfiram for married clients. A 'no treatment' control was not included in this study, but the results for married clients were so impressive and so superior to any published rates of spontaneous remission among those with serious alcohol problems, that it is reasonable to conclude that supervised disulfiram is an effective treatment for married alcoholics. Moreover, although the follow-up in this study was only six months, the superiority of the community reinforcement approach, in which supervised disulfiram was an essential part, was shown to extend to two years in the earlier study by Azrin (1976).

The evidence from the Azrin studies is supplemented by that from several other pieces of research described above (Bourne *et al*, 1966; Gerrein *et al*, 1973; Haynes, 1973; Bigelow *et al*, 1976; Liebson *et al*, 1978; Robichaud *et al*, 1979; Brewer & Smith, 1983; Sereny *et al*, 1986). None of these studies constituted a randomised, controlled trial of supervised disulfiram but, in the real world of providing treatment, it is unrealistic to confine attention to 'ideal' treatment trials. Rather, all the studies cited contribute, in different ways, to an accumulation of evidence on the basis on which a judgement of effectiveness can be based. Particularly impressive is the evidence relating to effectiveness among clients with the reputations of being difficult to treat – chronic drunkenness offenders or skid-row alcoholics (Bourne *et al*, 1966; Haynes, 1973; Brewer & Smith, 1983), heroin addicts (Liebson *et al*, 1978), and those who had already failed in treatment by other methods (Sereny *et al*, 1986). Much of this evidence is of the 'patients as their own controls' type – that is, where there is objective evidence of significantly inferior drinking status for substantial periods of time before the effects of the disulfiram intervention or clear evidence of repeated failures with other types of treatment. Again, in the real world of treatment evaluation, an accumulation of such evidence must carry some weight.

This is not to say that the field would not benefit from properly conducted, randomised, controlled trials of supervised disulfiram, using a large sample of patients, comparing it with unsupervised disulfiram and other types of control – similar to the multicentre trial reported by Fuller *et al* (1986) for unsupervised disulfiram. On the contrary, such trials are urgently needed. It is interesting to note that Fuller (1987) proposed such a study for funding but that his proposal was rejected.

In fact Chick *et al* (1992) have now published the results of a multicentre randomised partially blind six-month follow-up study involving 126 patients who received either 200 mg of disulfiram daily or 100 mg of vitamin C daily under the supervision of a nominated informant. A variety of estimates of alcohol consumption by patients, informants, clinicians and independent assessors ''generally showed significant differences in favour of disulfiram''. Perhaps the most impressive result was a significantly greater improvement in serum gamma glutamyl transpeptidase in the disulfiram group. Two-thirds of the disulfiram group asked if they could continue disulfiram treatment beyond the study period. The authors note that some patients did not experience a reaction after drinking alcohol. Five patients had their dose of disulfiram increased because of the lack of reaction and it is possible that the results might have been even more impressive had higher doses been used.

Why is disulfiram treatment unpopular?

In view of the above conclusion, it might be wondered why disulfiram treatment, at least in its supervised form, is not more popular among treatment providers. The issue was discussed by Brewer (1990), whose list of reasons included:

(a) the influence of Alcoholics Anonymous, who regard disulfiram pejoratively as a 'crutch'
(b) the influence of psychoanalysis and the search for underlying psychodynamic mechanisms
(c) exaggerated fears of side-effects and the DER
(d) professional rivalries in the alcohol problems field and anti-medical sentiment
(e) fears that the supervision of medication will cause conflict between patient and spouse
(f) vested financial interests in long-term in-patient treatment for alcoholism, which are incompatible with the out-patient use of disulfiram.

To this list should be added the fact that good evidence for the effectiveness of supervised disulfiram was not available for some time (see Azrin *et al*, 1982) and that it takes time for evidence to disseminate. I would agree with Brewer, however, that there has been some resistance to the acceptance of this evidence, even allowing for the generally irrational nature of the relationship between research evidence and treatment practice. One of the more important reasons for this resistance is contained in Brewer's fourth point above. In the UK, at least in recent years, there has been a process of 'demedicalisation' of the treatment response to alcohol problems and a growing prominence of the ideas and methods of other professions, particularly psychologists. It is plausible to suggest that disulfiram treatment has been unpopular because it is thought of as a highly 'medical' type of treatment, and has therefore run counter to the strong anti-medical tendency just described.

However, it is equally plausible to suggest that disulfiram should not be seen as a medical treatment, but as a form of behavioural intervention. What can be said immediately is that this is why supervised disulfiram treatment does not look out of place in Miller & Hester's (1986) list of effective treatments, which are all, of course, forms of behavioural intervention. The only thing which is 'medical' about disulfiram is the fact that it legally requires a medical qualification to prescribe and monitor its use.

Why does disulfiram work?

When disulfiram works, it does so by changing the patient's behaviour. But it is equally obvious that this change in behaviour is not accomplished because the pharmacological basis for behaviour has been changed. Rather than a psychopharmacological explanation of its action, we must seek a behavioural explanation of why disulfiram works when it does.

There are at least three ways of seeing disulfiram as a behavioural intervention. Firstly, it could be seen as a form of classical (or Pavlovian) conditioning in which an aversive reaction to alcohol is produced by the pairing of alcohol effects with the aversive unconditioned stimulus of the DER. Indeed, this was proposed as the basis for disulfiram's action in the early days of its use. This explanation assumes either that at least one challenge dose is given at the commencement of treatment to demonstrate to the patient the severity of the DER or that the patient has voluntarily drunk alcohol and risked the DER during the course of treatment.

This explanation is unlikely, however, precisely because challenge doses are rarely used in modern disulfiram treatment, yet all the evidence for its effectiveness comes from relatively modern research. Moreover, there is little evidence to suggest that patients who have drunk while on disulfiram do any better than those who have not. The study by Fuller & Roth (1979) clearly showed that it was the *deterrent* effect of disulfiram which was crucial.

This deterrent effect gives the clue to a much more likely behavioural explanation. This is that disulfiram treatment is a form of operant conditioning, and that disulfiram works because it alters the reinforcement contingencies applying to drinking. The operant model of drinking behaviour assumes that drinking occurs because, for the individual drinker, its positively reinforcing consequences outweigh its punishing consequences, including the situation in which short-term positive reinforcers are more powerful than longer-term negative consequences. Drinking will not occur when negative consequences are greater than positive. If this model is accepted, it is clear that disulfiram works by radically increasing the immediate punishing effects of drinking. This explanation makes it more understandable that disulfiram should appeal to Skinnerian theorists like Azrin and fit so well with the community reinforcement approach based on operant principles. It is important to note that it is not necessary for the individual to drink and experience the punishing consequences for this form of operant conditioning to be effective; all that is required is that the individual is aware of the altered reinforcement contingencies.

The problem with this explanation of disulfiram's effects is that, if valid, it cannot account for the maintenance of behavioural change after the altered reinforcement contingencies are no longer in effect – in plainer language, it predicts a relapse after the patient has stopped taking disulfiram. In this connection, it is interesting to note that the rate of alcohol-related absenteeism in Robichaud *et al*'s (1979) study returned nearly to baseline after disulfiram treatment ended. Indeed, this is a frequently voiced criticism of this treatment. One solution is clearly to continue giving disulfiram for the rest of the patient's life, but many would consider this undesirable.

One possible way in which disulfiram treatment might effect longer-term changes has been suggested by Brewer (1988). This point of view regards it as a form of cue exposure with response prevention, similar in many ways to methods used to treat phobic and obsessive–compulsive disorders. The idea is that disulfiram enables the patient to confront situations where there would normally be a high risk of relapse, while forcibly preventing drinking from taking place. As a result, craving responses associated with external and internal stimuli are extinguished and the patient's self-efficacy (i.e. his/her confidence that the high-risk situation can be coped with without resorting to drinking) is increased.

This is an ingenious hypothesis and, if valid, would offer an explanation of how disulfiram might result in behavioural changes outlasting the disulfiram treatment. However, there are two problems with this hypothesis. Firstly, it is possible that the extinction of conditioned craving responses only takes place when the consummatory response (i.e. drinking) is available. In other words, the individual must be exposed to temptation for extinction to occur, and the knowledge that disulfiram has been taken removes, or at least considerably reduces, temptation. Secondly, it is possible that, for self-efficacy to be increased in the manner suggested by the hypothesis, the patient must be able to attribute the success of coping efforts in the high-risk situation to him/herself. When disulfiram has been taken, the credit for coping is attributed to an external agency (i.e. the disulfiram). However, Brewer's hypothesis and the two objections to it are eminently researchable among patients undergoing disulfiram treatment.

Even if the cue exposure hypothesis of disulfiram's action is incorrect, it is likely that the least disulfiram does is to offer a breathing space and a respite from the ravages of heavy drinking – an improvement in physical health and a break in the vicious circle of problems and drinking. However, we need more research into what happens after disulfiram treatment has ended and firmer evidence that some of the changes introduced by disulfiram are permanent or at least of longer duration than the treatment itself.

References

ARMOR, D. J., POLICH, J. M. & STAMBUL, H. B. (1978) *Alcoholism and Treatment*. New York: Wiley.

AZRIN, N. H. (1976) Improvements in the community-reinforcement approach to alcoholism. *Behaviour Research and Therapy*, **14**, 339–348.

—— , SISSON, R. W., MEYERS, R., *et al* (1982) Alcoholism treatment by disulfiram and community reinforcement therapy. *Journal of Behavior Therapy and Experimental Psychiatry*, **13**, 105–112.

BAEKELAND, F., LUNDWALL, L., KISSIN, B., *et al* (1971) Correlates of outcome in disulfiram treatment of alcoholism. *Journal of Nervous and Mental Disease*, **153**, 1–9.

BERGSTROM, B., OHLIN, H., LINDBLOM, P. E., *et al* (1982) Is disulfiram implantation effective? *Lancet*, **i**, 49–50.

BIGELOW, G., STRICKLER, D., LIEBSON, I., *et al* (1976) Maintaining disulfiram ingestion among out-patient alcoholics: a security-deposit contingency contracting procedure. *Behaviour Research and Therapy*, **14**, 378–381.

BOURNE, P. G., ALFORD, J. A. & BOWCOCK, J. Z. (1966) Treatment of skid-row alcoholics with disulfiram. *Quarterly Journal of Studies on Alcohol*, **27**, 42–48.

BREWER, C. (1987) Disulfiram treatment for alcoholism. (Letter to the editor.) *Journal of the American Medical Association*, **257**, 926.

—— (1988) The management of opiate abuse: learning from other addictions. *Journal of Drug Issues*, **18**, 679–697.

—— (1990) Combining pharmacological antagonists and behavioural psychotherapy in treating addictions: Why it is effective but unpopular. *British Journal of Psychiatry*, **157**, 34–44.

—— & SMITH, J. (1983) Probation linked supervised disulfiram in the treatment of habitual drunken offenders: results of a pilot study. *British Medical Journal*, **287**, 1282–1283.

CHICK, J., RITSON, B., CONNAUGHTON, J., *et al* (1988) Advice versus treatment for alcoholism: a controlled trial. *British Journal of Addiction*, **83**, 159–170.

—— , GOUGH, K., WOJCIECH, F., *et al* (1992) Disulfiram treatment of alcoholism. *British Journal of Psychiatry*, **161**, 84–89.

EMRICK, C. D. (1975) A review of psychologically oriented treatment of alcoholism. II. The relative effectiveness of different treatment approaches and the effectiveness of treatment versus no treatment. *Journal of Studies on Alcohol*, **36**, 88–108.

FULLER, R. K. (1987) Disulfiram treatment for alcoholism. (Letter to the editor.) *Journal of the American Medical Association*, **257**, 927.

—— & ROTH, H. P. (1979) Disulfiram for the treatment of alcoholism: an evaluation in 128 men. *Annals of Internal Medicine*, **90**, 901–904.

—— & WILLIFORD, W. O. (1980) Life-table analysis of abstinence in a study evaluating the efficacy of disulfiram. *Alcoholism: Clinical and Experimental Research*, **4**, 298–301.

—— & NEIDERHISER, D. H. (1981) Evaluation and application of a urinary diethylamine method to measure compliance with disulfiram therapy. *Journal of Studies on Alcohol*, **42**, 202–207.

—— , ROTH, H. & LONG, S. (1983) Compliance with disulfiram treatment of alcoholism. *Journal of Chronic Diseases*, **36**, 161–170.

——, BRANCHEY, L., BRIGHTWELL, D. R., *et al* (1986) Disulfiram treatment of alcoholism: a Veterans Administration cooperative study. *Journal of the American Medical Association*, **256**, 1449–1455.

GERARD, D. L. & SAENGER, G. (1966) *Out-Patient Treatment of Alcoholism: A Study of Outcome and its Determinants*. Toronto: University of Toronto Press.

GERREIN, J. R., ROSENBERG, C. M. & MANOHAR, V. (1973) Disulfiram maintenance in out-patient treatment of alcoholism. *Archives of General Psychiatry*, **28**, 798–802.

GORDIS, E. & PETERSON, K. (1977) Disulfiram therapy in alcoholism: patient compliance studied with a urine-detection procedure. *Alcoholism: Clinical and Experimental Research*, **1**, 213–216.

HAYNES, S. (1973) Contingency management in a municipally-administered antabuse program for alcoholics. *Journal of Behaviour Therapy and Experimental Psychiatry*, **4**, 31–32.

HOFF, E. C. (1961) The use of pharmacological adjuncts in the psychotherapy of alcoholics. *Quarterly Journal of Studies on Alcohol*, **22** (suppl. 1), 138–150.

HUNT, G. M. & AZRIN, N. H. (1973) A community-reinforcement approach to alcoholism. *Behaviour Research and Therapy*, **11**, 91–104.

JOHNSEN, J., STOWELL, A., BACHE-WIIG, J. E., *et al* (1987) A double-blind placebo controlled study of male alcoholics given a subcutaneous disulfiram implantation. *British Journal of Addiction*, **82**, 607–613.

KEANE, T. M., FOY, D. W., NUNN, B., *et al* (1984) Spouse contracting to increase antabuse compliance in alcoholic veterans. *Journal of Clinical Psychology*, **40**, 340–344.

KOFOED, L. L. (1987) Chemical monitoring of disulfiram compliance: a study of alcoholic outpatients. *Alcoholism: Clinical and Experimental Research*, **11**, 481–485.

LIEBSON, I. & BIGELOW, G. (1972) A behavioural-pharmacological treatment of dually addicted patients. *Behaviour Research and Therapy*, **10**, 403–405.

——, —— & FLAMER, R. (1973) Alcoholism among methadone patients: a specific treatment method. *American Journal of Psychiatry*, **130**, 483–485.

——, TOMMASELLO, A. & BIGELOW, G. G. (1978) A behavioral treatment of alcoholic methadone patients. *Annals of Internal Medicine*, **89**, 342–344.

LISKOW, B. I. & GOODWIN, D. W. (1987) Pharmacological treatment of alcohol intoxication, withdrawal and dependence: a critical review. *Journal of Studies on Alcohol*, **48**, 356–370.

MILLER, W. R. & HESTER, R. K. (1980) Treating the problem drinker: Modern approaches. In *The Addictive Behaviors: Treatment of Alcoholism, Drug Abuse, Smoking and Obesity* (ed. W. R. Miller), pp. 11–141. Oxford: Pergamon Press.

—— & —— (1986) The effectiveness of alcoholism treatment: what research reveals. In *Treating Addictive Behaviors: Processes of Change* (eds W. R. Miller & N. Heather), pp. 121–174. New York: Plenum Press.

MORLAND, J., JOHNSEN, J., BACHE-WIIG, J. E., *et al* (1984) Lack of pharmacological effects of implanted disulfiram. In *Pharmacological Treatments for Alcoholism* (eds G. Edwards & J. Littleton), pp. 573–578. New York: Methuen.

O'FARRELL, T. J., CUTTER, H. S. G. & FLOYD, F. J. (1985) Evaluating behavioral marital therapy for male alcoholics: effects on marital adjustment and communication from before to after treatment. *Behavior Therapy*, **16**, 147–167.

—— & BAYOG, R. D. (1986) Antabuse contracts for married alcoholics and their spouses: a method to maintain antabuse ingestion and decrease conflict about drinking. *Journal of Substance Abuse Treatment*, **3**, 1–8.

PAULSON, S. M., KRAUSE, S. & IBER, F. L. (1977) Development and evaluation of a compliance test for patients taking disulfiram. *Johns Hopkins Medical Journal*, **141**, 119–125.

ROBICHAUD, C., STRICKLER, D., BIGELOW, G., *et al* (1979) Disulfiram maintenance employee alcoholism treatment: a three-phase evaluation. *Behaviour Research and Therapy*, **17**, 618–621.

RYCHTARIK, R. G., SMITH, P. O., JONES, S. L., *et al* (1983) Assessing disulfiram compliance: validation study of an abbreviated breath test procedure. *Addictive Behaviors*, **8**, 361–368.

SERENY, G., SHARMA, V., HOLT, J., *et al* (1986) Mandatory supervised antabuse therapy in an out-patient alcoholism program: a pilot study. *Alcoholism: Clinical and Experimental Research*, **10**, 290–292.

WALLERSTEIN, R. S., CHOTLOS, J. W., FRIEND, M. B., *et al* (1957) *Hospital Treatment of Alcoholism: A Comparative Experimental Study*. New York: Basic Books.
WEXBERG, L. E. (1953) The out-patient treatment of alcoholism in the District of Columbia. *Quarterly Journal of Studies on Alcohol*, **14**, 514–524.
WILSON, A. (1975) Disulfiram implantation in alcoholism treatment: a review. *Journal of Studies on Alcohol*, **36**, 555–565.
——, DAVIDSON, W. J. & WHITE, J. (1976) Disulfiram implantation: placebo, psychological deterrent, and pharmacological deterrent effects. *British Journal of Psychiatry*, **129**, 277–280.

2 Disulfiram and behaviour therapy: a social–biochemical model of alcohol abuse and treatment

NATHAN H. AZRIN

As a psychologist, not a doctor, I approached the problem of alcoholism from the perspective of treating the disorder by psychological means. The results of the initial study (Hunt & Azrin, 1973) using community-reinforcement therapy (CRT) were quite favourable, but the procedure used was so onerous that other therapeutic factors were sought, among which was disulfiram. So promising were the results obtained then that a separate analysis was undertaken of the separate and combined effects of disulfiram and psychological procedures (Azrin *et al*, 1982). The product of this was the discovery that both methods were effective, but with different types of alcoholic patients, and only if disulfiram was administered in a manner at variance with usual usage.

At the beginning of this work, alcoholism was conceptualised in learning theory terms as a problem resulting from excessive use of a reinforcer, ethanol. The sources of reinforcement for alcohol were conceptualised as:

(a) the intrinsic reinforcing nature of ethanol itself, enhanced by its characteristics as an addictive substance which produce tolerance, thereby requiring progressively greater amounts to provide the same effect, together with the aversive properties of the withdrawal symptoms upon discontinuation of drinking
(b) the taste factors, emphasised by the manufacturers to promote its use
(c) its virtual requirement for use at culturally prescribed occasions such as weddings, celebrations, sports events, cocktail parties
(d) its required use as part of many social and peer groups
(e) its enhanced reinforcing properties during periods of interpersonal stress and psychological tension.

With such potent and diverse sources of strength as a reinforcer from chemical, cultural, social, and emotional influences, this analysis predicted that there would be virtually universal alcoholism without equally potent

19

countervailing influences, that is, the negative consequences of drinking. Such inhibitory influences were conceptualised as being primarily forms of time-out from positive reinforcers that would otherwise be available. Interference with extended or excessive drinking results in:

(a) maintaining employment and financial independence
(b) continuing a marital relationship
(c) participating in customary recreational and social activities
(d) medical well-being.

The factors listed as reinforcers are all fairly immediate: taste, avoidance of withdrawal symptoms, social approval, and reduction of tension, whereas the inhibitory factors all are uncertain or delayed. This differential delay between positive and negative consequences could partly explain the emergence of excessive drinking. Further, the deterrent effect of the negative consequences could no longer be expected to be effective as a time-out from reinforcers, once the alcoholic had reached the extreme stage of alcoholism in which the vocational, marital, social and recreational reinforcers were absent. Time-out from reinforcement is not possible when reinforcement is absent.

This analysis of reinforcement suggested that treatment might consist of re-establishing or strengthening the natural deterrents to drinking by providing counselling for job finding, marital dysfunction, recreational pursuits, and interpersonal social skills. Because of this combination of community and reinforcement concepts, the method was designated the community-reinforcement method of alcoholism treatment.

The initial study (Hunt & Azrin, 1973) using this method was conducted with 16 chronic alcoholics, all of whom were in-patients in a state hospital, divided randomly into two closely matched groups. One group, the 'traditional' one, served as the controls and received the usual hospital treatment of group therapy, AA counselling, individual supportive counselling, and educational programmes regarding alcoholism. The other group, the community-reinforcement patients, received counselling in job-finding, marital counselling, priming of recreational activities, and interpersonal communication and social skills training. The results, shown in Fig. 2.1, were fairly dramatic, in that seven out of the eight subjects treated by community-reinforcement became virtually abstinent and regained normal marital, social, and vocational functioning. Of the eight alcoholics treated by the traditional in-patient hospital programme, all but one resumed heavy drinking, and were found during the same six-month follow-up period to have continued drinking, to be unemployed and absent from their home, as well as being frequently admitted to hospital or other institutions for alcohol-related activities.

However, in spite of the gratifying results that were obtained, the community-reinforcement method required an excessive amount of counselling

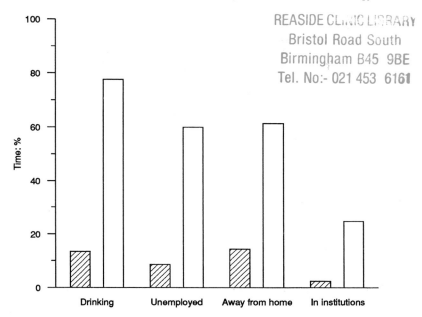

Fig. 2.1. A comparison of the key dependent measures for the reinforcement (▨) and control (☐) groups (n = 16) since discharge: mean percentages of time spent drinking, unemployed, away from home and in institutions (source Hunt & Azrin, 1973)

time – averaging 50 hours per patient. Therefore, several procedures were added to reduce dependence on the counsellor, such as group counselling and a 'buddy' system which used former successful patients as therapist-assistants. Notably, disulfiram was also added as a means of providing a negative consequence that would be more immediate than the long-delayed negative consequences otherwise operative naturally.

Studies of disulfiram up to that time had not been generally favourable (Ludwig *et al*, 1970; Lubetkin *et al*, 1971). Indeed, why should the alcoholic ingest a substance which would interfere with the immediate reinforcement normally produced by drinking? The problem was seen as one of treatment-compliance or medication-adherence, in which ingestion of the medication would be supervised by a partner in a manner that maximised adherence.

Some of the rules developed for the assured use of disulfiram are outlined below.

(a) Identify a disulfiram monitor who would be substantially and negatively affected by resumption of drinking, e.g. spouse, family member, employer, lover, landlord.

(b) The monitor should normally have regular, ideally daily, contact with the alcoholic.

B

(c) Specify precisely the time and place where the disulfiram could be taken conveniently, with both persons present.

(d) Have disulfiram taken at a time when other forms of medication are normally taken, i.e. the 'response-chaining' principle.

(e) Grind up the disulfiram tablet and dissolve it in a drink (coffee, tea, juice) to avoid any suspicion of later expulsion.

(f) If the monitor is not present when the patient has taken the disulfiram, the patient should take another tablet that same day, when the monitor is present, to provide absolute assurance to the monitor.

(g) The patient should thank the monitor for taking the time to observe.

(h) The monitor should comment on some positive attribute of the patient that is associated with sobriety, i.e. job status, love by children, doing chores, financial security.

(i) At each therapeutic session, the monitor attends with the patient, if possible, so that the therapist can instruct, supervise, and provide feedback to both.

(j) At each therapeutic session, the disulfiram is taken in the presence of the therapist.

(k) The monitor is to telephone the therapist if the patient omits taking disulfiram for three days; the therapist then telephones the patient to arrange a session.

(l) When the usual 30-day supply of tablets is near-depleted, the monitor prompts and assists the patient to renew the prescription; failure to do so has been one of the most apparent major causes of discontinuing disulfiram.

(m) The therapist asks the patient and monitor to rehearse probable situations which cause the reluctance to take the disulfiram, and teaches them how to overcome such interferences.

(n) The patient is taught to view the use and ritual of taking disulfiram as a means of providing assurance to himself and his loved ones that he will not succumb to temptations that are otherwise beyond his control. It is emphasised that the central feature is the patient's desire, not coercion.

(o) The disulfiram dosage is the minimal one (usually 250 mg) that will produce an adverse reaction yet not seriously jeopardise health. Larger doses may well provide more interference with drinking, but often lead to greater reluctance to continue and possible discontinuation. It was considered preferable to permit the occasional or reduced level of drinking than to risk serious medical complications or discontinuation of the medication.

(p) If the patient is reluctant to accept disulfiram as a continuing regime, a short-term trial is encouraged for any period that is acceptable – even one week initially.

(q) If the patient refuses to initiate disulfiram for any period of time, because of the conviction that control will be possible without it, the therapist considers negotiating an agreement that the patient will definitely initiate usage immediately on the next occasion of inebriation.

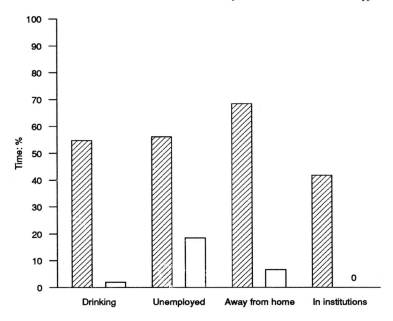

Fig. 2.2. Comparison of the community-reinforcement clients (□) and the control clients (▧) on each of four measures. The 'drinking' measure designates the percentage of days on which the client was drinking alcohol. The 'unemployed' measure designates the percentage of days on which the client did not work. 'Away from home' designates the percentage of days the client was absent from his family or home. 'In institutions' designates the time spent in a mental hospital or prison. The period of time for the data was the first six months after discharge of the client from the hospital (source Azrin, 1976)

The results of a study (Azrin, 1976) incorporating the group format, buddy system, and use of disulfiram, as described above, were again favourable. As seen in Fig. 2.2, the patients receiving this modified reinforcement programme drank on 2% of the post-discharge days against 55% for the matched control patients. As in the previous study (Hunt & Azrin, 1973), the reinforcement patients were employed, remained at home, and were not incarcerated for more time than the control patients.

The principal objective of the revised reinforcement programme was to decrease counselling time. The data showed that this was indeed reduced – from a mean of 50 hours to a mean of 30 hours, which is a large decrease (40%), but still represents a substantial duration of professional time in absolute terms.

A third study (Azrin *et al*, 1982) was conducted, but this time using out-patients rather than in-patients, since admission to hospital itself seemed to sever the vocational, family, marital, and social influences which the community-reinforcement procedures were designed to strengthen. This study further assessed the effect of the supervised disulfiram procedure when

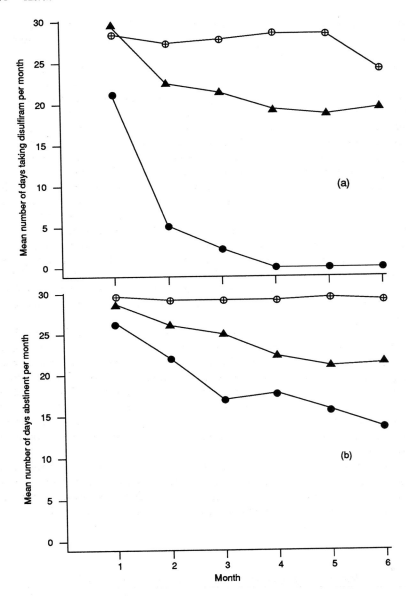

Fig. 2.3.   Mean no. of days on which (a) disulfiram was taken during each month (30 days) of the six months of follow-up by 43 patients and (b) mean no. of days on which drinking occurred each month (30 days) of the six months of follow-up. Disulfiram was given in the usual manner in the 'traditional' group (—●—) whereas adherence was socially motivated for the 'disulfiram assurance' group (—▲—). The 'behaviour therapy' group (—⊕—) received community-orientated reinforcement therapy in addition to the disulfiram assurance programme (source Azrin et al, 1982)

used alone, without the behaviour (reinforcement) therapy, and compared it with disulfiram used in the traditional manner, as well as when used in combination with the behaviour therapy.

Figure 2.3(a) shows the mean number of days per month on which the patients took the disulfiram, for each of the three treatment conditions. Under the 'traditional' method of prescribing, disulfiram usage decreased sharply after the first month to a zero level after three months. In contrast, use of disulfiram continued at a high rate – about 20 days/month when the special 'disulfiram assurance' procedure was used. This finding shows that the special disulfiram procedure described above is a fairly effective method for assuring that out-patients will make use of this medication.

Figure 2.3(b) shows how drinking was affected in this same study. The results showed that the patients receiving disulfiram in the 'traditional' manner were abstinent on progressively fewer days during each succeeding month, such that they were abstinent on only 13 days during the sixth month. In contrast, the patients whose sole treatment was taking disulfiram in the special 'disulfiram assurance' manner were abstinent for about 22 days per month at six months. These results constitute one of the first published findings that in a normal out-patient setting, disulfiram can have a beneficial clinical outcome, the stipulation being that special monitoring procedures are required.

The data from this study also demonstrate the results of the behaviour therapy programme – which included both the special disulfiram assurance procedure and the community-reinforcement counselling. It will be seen from Fig. 2.3(a) that this behaviour therapy programme resulted in fairly constant use of disulfiram, averaging about 27 days per month, and also resulted in almost total abstinence for the six months (Fig. 2.3(b)). These results demonstrate that the psychological counselling greatly increased the effect of the disulfiram assurance procedure, when the two were used in combination.

The data from this study reveal that the patients' marital status was a major determinant of whether the disulfiram procedure was effective or not. Table 2.1 shows that for single persons, the disulfiram assurance procedure produced no increase in abstinence, but, surprisingly, produced complete

TABLE 2.1
Mean number of days abstinent during the sixth month (30 days) of follow-up

	Singles	Couples
Traditional	6.75	17.4
Disulfiram assurance	8.0	30.0
Behaviour therapy plus disulfiram assurance	28.3	30.0

From Azrin *et al* (1982).

abstinence (30 days per month) for those alcoholics who were part of a couple. This finding suggests that for married or cohabiting alcoholics, psychological counselling is unnecessary: the disulfiram assurance procedure alone was sufficient to produce near-total abstinence. The brief time needed to implement this latter procedure gives this finding great practical significance.

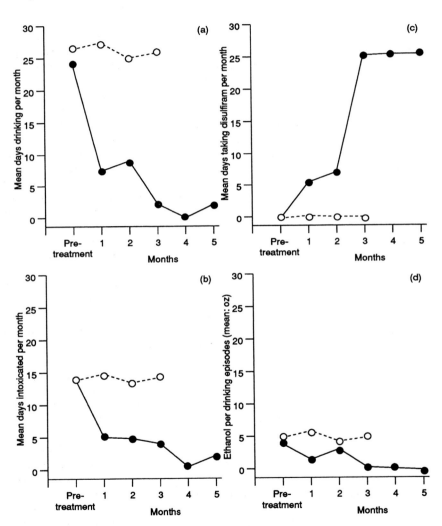

Fig. 2.4.   Mean scores (n = 12) for (a) the number of days drinking, (b) number of days intoxicated, (c) number of days taking disulfiram and (d) amount of alcohol per drinking episode for the alcoholic family member for two different treatment conditions, traditional (--○--) and reinforcement (—●—). Each data point is the mean during successive months of treatment (source Sisson & Azrin, 1986)

On the other hand, for the single, unattached alcoholics, the data (Table 2.1) show that in addition to assured disulfiram, the behaviour therapy was in fact necessary. This combination again resulted in near-total abstinence – 28.3 days abstinent per month for these single persons.

Since a common problem in treating alcoholics is their refusal to seek treatment, an additional study (Sisson & Azrin, 1986) was carried out to reduce drinking by alcoholics who refused to enter treatment, but whose family members (wife, sibling, parent, child) requested assistance in coping with the drinking person. In this study, the family members were taught several tactics for reducing the stress to the family that was caused by the drinking problem; but they were also educated regarding disulfiram and how they might influence the alcoholic to enter that treatment. This reinforcement approach was contrasted with a traditional approach with a randomly assigned group of family members, who received traditional counselling from self-help groups.

Figure 2.4 shows that before treatment, the alcoholics in both groups averaged about 25 drinking days per month. In traditionally treated families, the patients continued at this high rate of drinking during the next four months of treatment, whereas drinking decreased monthly to about three days per month for the reinforcement-counselled families. It will also be seen that the reinforcement-counselled families had fewer days of intoxication, consumed less ethanol per drinking episode, and had fairly consistent use of disulfiram, in contrast with the alcoholics in the traditionally counselled families.

These studies provide potentially useful clinical tools for treating alcoholism, and support the following conclusions:

(a) disulfiram prescribed in the usual unmonitored manner does not reduce drinking in an out-patient situation

(b) a large, clinically important reduction of drinking does result from training a monitor to supervise and assure continued disulfiram ingestion

(c) for alcoholics who have a close family (particularly marital) relationship, the disulfiram assurance procedure is sufficient to produce sobriety, with no benefit added by psychological treatment; for such married alcoholics, the initiation of sobriety by the disulfiram seems to allow the strong natural deterrents against drinking to function

(d) for alcoholics with no close family ties, the disulfiram procedure alone, monitored or traditional, is ineffective in reducing drinking; psychological treatment by behaviour therapy is then necessary, in addition to the disulfiram assurance procedure

(e) for alcoholics who do not seek treatment, concerned family members can be counselled to promote the initiation of treatment by this combined disulfiram–behaviour therapy approach. Once such treatment has been initiated, drinking is reduced.

These studies support the view of alcoholism as an interactive social–biochemical problem.

Success is possible by biochemical (pharmacological) means alone when the social bonds are present, but when these bonds are absent, combining psychological treatment with pharmacological is generally effective in producing sobriety. This combined approach is possible even when the family member, rather than the alcoholic, initially requests the assistance. At the clinical level, these results suggest that a team approach by doctors and psychologists can use the available pharmacological and psychological treatments in a combined manner, to the greatest advantage.

References

AZRIN, N. H. (1976) Improvements in the community-reinforcement approach to alcoholism. *Behaviour Research and Therapy*, **14**, 339–348.
——, SISSON, R. W., MEYERS, R., *et al* (1982) Alcoholism treatment by disulfiram and community reinforcement therapy. *Journal of Behaviour Therapy and Experimental Psychiatry*, **13**, 105–112.
HUNT, G. M. & AZRIN, N. H. (1973) A community-reinforcement approach to alcoholism. *Behaviour Research and Therapy*, **11**, 91–104.
LUDWIG, A. W., LEVINE, J. & STARK, L. H. (1970) *LSD and Alcoholism*. Springfield, Illinois: Thomas.
LUBETKIN, B. S., RIVERS, P. C. & ROSENBERG, C. M. (1971) Difficulties of disulfiram therapy with alcoholics. *Quarterly Journal of Studies on Alcohol*, **32**, 118–171.
SISSON, R. W. & AZRIN, N. H. (1986) Family-member involvement to initiate and promote treatment of problem drinkers. *Journal of Behaviour Therapy and Experimental Psychiatry*, **17**, 15–21.

3 What the textbooks say about disulfiram: a review of recent publications

COLIN BREWER

Although disulfiram, when taken under supervision, is a treatment whose effectiveness in controlled trials has been repeatedly and consistently demonstrated (Miller, 1989; Brewer, 1992; Heather, Chapter 1) its use in the management of alcohol abuse is far from being universally accepted. Most of the research in this field was published before 1983. Indeed, only one further randomised controlled study (with positive findings) has been published since then (Chick *et al*, 1992).

Of the older studies, the work of Azrin *et al* is particularly convincing and has been praised by several authorities for its experimental design and the comprehensive nature of the community-reinforcement therapy (CRT) approach. However, some of these authorities have virtually ignored the inclusion of disulfiram in CRT, even though the researchers themselves regarded it as a very important and cost-effective component:

> "Among married clients, supervised Antabuse was sufficient to produce nearly complete abstinence. These clients usually obtained jobs and re-established satisfying marital and social relationships with no assistance from the counsellor." (Azrin *et al*, 1982)

It is difficult to know which sources of information have the most influence on the choice of treatment in a particular field. Fashion, tradition, publicity (good or bad), as well as commendation or criticism by prominent practitioners doubtless play a part, but in a speciality which aspires to a scientific orientation, knowledge of the research literature should surely play an important role. Many competent and well informed practitioners, like many students, do not feel it necessary to read all the relevant journals; they rely on textbooks, believing that these will accurately and fairly summarise important areas of knowledge at the time the book was written or revised. This chapter compares the advice about disulfiram given in a representative selection of recent textbooks.

A major international addiction conference in Glasgow in August 1992 provided the material, since among the exhibition stands was an academic bookstall at which I examined all the textbooks on display whose titles indicated that they were concerned with the treatment of alcohol abuse or with addictions in general. Titles which indicated concern solely with solvents, tranquillisers, opiates, or other illicit drugs were excluded. Sixteen textbooks met the criteria for inclusion.

Method

For each book, I first counted the index entries for disulfiram and related headings such as Antabuse, Abstem, calcium carbimide, or alcohol-sensitising drugs. If the index contained no such entries, I read through any chapters on treatment or relapse-prevention to see if disulfiram was mentioned. Both the amount of space devoted to disulfiram and the book's advice about the place of disulfiram in treatment were noted, as were any journal references to disulfiram, particularly to controlled studies. In the light of Heather's extensive literature review (Chapter 1), it seemed superfluous to review *Controlled Drinking* by Heather & Robertson (1990).

Results

Three categories emerged, and the textbooks are grouped accordingly.

(a) Textbooks which discuss disulfiram but do not stress the importance of supervision or contain up-to-date references to controlled trials of supervised disulfiram

A Manual for Chemical Dependence (Ciraulo & Shader, 1990)

There are five index references to disulfiram, and one to calcium carbimide. There is a very detailed discussion of disulfiram with related drugs and a reference to the need, in some cases, to increase the dose to 500 mg daily, but the authors do not mention the need for supervision. They conclude: "Despite a number of studies and clinical reports, questions remain concerning the efficacy and risks of disulfiram". However, there are no references to the work of Azrin or to any other controlled trial of supervised disulfiram.

Concise Guide to Treatment of Alcoholism and Addictions (Frances & Franklin, 1989)

There is one index reference to disulfiram, and two pages of discussion. The antipathy of many Alcoholics Anonymous groups to disulfiram is noted.

"Disulfiram has been shown to be useful in certain subtypes. Older, socially stable alcoholics, affluent, married, less sociopathic patients, who tend to be compulsive, do better on disulfiram." Although the authors state that "It can be administered in an oral suspension", there is no mention of the importance of supervision. Disulfiram does not appear in any of the 37 references at the end of the chapter.

The International Handbook of Addiction Behaviour (Glass, 1991)

There are two index entries for disulfiram, and three pages of discussion in a chapter by J. Peachey, 'Detoxification & pharmacotherapy'. Differences between disulfiram and calcium carbimide are summarised. "The fear of experiencing the reaction [with alcohol] is usually a sufficient deterrent to prevent drinking; experiencing the reaction strengthens the patient's resolve not to drink . . . The alcohol-sensitizing drugs are used for patients when the treatment goal is abstinence and there are no major medical problems." Although the discussion is detailed and quite favourable, the importance of supervision is not mentioned and there are no references to any of the controlled studies.

(b) Textbooks which do not mention disulfiram or touch on it only briefly

Drugs and Addictive Behaviour: A Guide to Treatment (Ghodse, 1989)

There are no index entries for disulfiram and little discussion of alcohol abuse, though alcohol has two index entries. There is detailed description of methadone maintenance, but no mention of the use of disulfiram as an adjunct (Liebson *et al*, 1973).

Relapse and Addictive Behaviour (Gossop, 1989)

There are no index entries for disulfiram or carbimide. The chapter 'Relapse: A Critique', by B. Saunders & S. Alsop, does not mention the work of Azrin *et al*, which is surprising since Saunders (1985) has previously held up CRT as an exemplary approach and is aware that Azrin *et al* regard both disulfiram and supervision as important (Brewer, 1987).

A further chapter by A. Marlat & J. Gordon – 'Relapse Prevention; Future Directions' – criticises rigidity in treatment, especially "the ubiquitous 30 day in-patient treatment program favoured by many experts in the United States for a variety of addiction problems . . . [which] is a manifestation of this uniformity assumption".

Ironically, the authors then draw an analogy between hypertension and alcoholism treatments and specifically mention the need for medication if hypertension fails to respond to lifestyle changes. ''A similar graded series of interventions would seem appropriate for many addiction problems''. However, disulfiram is evidently not one of the graded interventions to be considered, although – even more ironically in view of their earlier criticism – ''if all else fails, the use of long term in-patient treatment programs can be implemented as a last resort''.

Marlat (personal communication) appears to have changed his views recently, and now recommends disulfiram as a relapse-prevention technique.

Alcohol Problems (Anderson et al, *1989)*

There are no index entries for alcohol-sensitising drugs. Although open discussion of relapses is encouraged, so that patients can recognise strategies for preventing a further recurrence, supervised disulfiram is not one of the strategies mentioned. Ironically, the book contains chapters on 'The Effectiveness of Intervention' and 'Audit and Research'.

Relapse Prevention for Addictive Behaviours, A Manual for Therapists (Wanigaratne et al, *1990)*

There are two index entries for alcohol-sensitising drugs. Disulfiram is mentioned in a single sentence in the chapter on 'High Risk Situations' as ''a strategy while on holiday . . . supervised by [the patient's] sister'', but there are no references to any studies involving supervision.

Alcohol, Social Work and Helping (Collins, 1990)

There are two index entries for disulfiram. In a brief discussion, it is described as ''this controversial deterrent drug . . . [which] has encouraged some general practitioners to offer community-based support even where detoxification is required. But there is legitimate concern that its use undermines the development of self-efficacy in the patient in the long term''. The book is very thoroughly referenced, but there are no references to controlled trials of supervised disulfiram or to any studies which would justify the author's ''legitimate concern''.

(c) Textbooks which emphasise supervision or refer to clinical trials of supervised disulfiram

Alcoholism, A Guide to Diagnosis, Intervention and Treatment (Gallant, 1987)

There are eight index entries for disulfiram and two for the disulfiram–ethanol reaction, and one reference to calcium carbimide. In 'The Use of Psycho-pharmacologic Medications in Alcoholism', there is a very detailed review.

"Having been medically responsible for administering Antabuse to more than 20,000 patients in the past 25 years, I have no doubt that the benefits of Antabuse far outweigh the risks of taking this medication. . . . On innumerable occasions, patients, after some discouraging experience, have said to me 'If it were not for Antabuse I would have drunk that day' [this] has made me realise what an invaluable help Antabuse has been to many of my patients. . . . There are some excellent, well controlled, scientific investigations which show the effectiveness of Antabuse and objectively confirm my subjective experiences. . . . It is clear, then, that Antabuse increases the therapeutic success rates of patients who are very difficult cases as well as the average alcoholic patients who are treated in an out-patient setting".

"Antabuse can be used not only to produce an adverse reaction to drinking alcohol but also as a symbol of the patient's commitment to treatment. . . . In our treatment approach, the spouse is asked to participate actively . . . by administering [it]."

However, although the unrandomised (though not unimpressive) study by Sereny *et al* (1986) is discussed, there are no references to other studies of supervised disulfiram.

Comprehensive Handbook of Drug and Alcohol Addiction (Miller, 1991)

There are five index references to disulfiram. It was the only book to discuss the usefulness of disulfiram in patients on methadone maintenance (Liebson *et al*, 1973): "Up to 25% of patients on methadone programs have been reported to have drinking problems".

"Disulfiram . . . becomes much more valuable when carefully integrated into work with the patient and network, particularly when taken under observation. . . . The administration of disulfiram under observation is a treatment option which is easily adapted to work with social networks. A patient who takes disulfiram cannot drink; a patient who agrees to be observed by a reasonable party while taking disulfiram will not miss his dose without the observer's knowing." However, there are no references to controlled trials in this context.

The Treatment of Drinking Problems: A Guide for the Helping Professions (Edwards, 1987)

There is one index entry for disulfiram and one for calcium carbimide. Disulfiram is mentioned, along with behaviour therapies and psychotherapy, in a chapter on 'Special Techniques'. It is a detailed discussion, making several important points. The author notes that the reaction with alcohol can be very variable in intensity, but no increase in dose is suggested if the reaction is too small.

The advice that "Patients with heart disease, cerebral vascular insufficiency, liver disease or diabetes should not be given these drugs" is perhaps excessively cautious, but Edwards several times refers to the importance of supervision. "The spouse may also have her anxieties much relieved by seeing her partner take the daily tablet. . . . A degree of acceptable supervision is set up (the tablet taken in the doctor's office for instance, or in the medical room at work, or under the eyes of the wife), or a contingency management plan or therapeutic contract established. Disulfiram has been used in this way within industrial treatment programmes and in the USA within court probation programmes."

Edwards believes that in many cases, "one of these substances should at least be offered, and the nature of the treatment explained. . . ." However, the statement that "Despite the many years during which these substances have been in use, it is still difficult to form a firm view as to their usefulness" is rather weakened by the absence of any references to controlled trials.

Understanding and Treating Alcoholism (vol. 2) (Littrell, 1991)

There are four index references to disulfiram and one mention of calcium carbimide in the text. There are four pages of discussion, and the attitude to disulfiram is one of moderate encouragement. However, the advice that it is "contraindicated in those with liver disease, coronary disease, diabetes, hypothyroidism and cerebral damage" is supported only by a single reference to authors who, like Littrell himself, are not medical, and he does not indicate whether the contraindications are relative or absolute. A single controlled study involving supervision (Gerrein *et al*, 1973) is cited, but there is no mention of Azrin's work. Neither is the need for supervision spelled out, although there are references to papers involving spouse contracting.

Counselling Problem Drinkers (Davidson et al, *1991)*

There are two index entries, and a very detailed and practical description of disulfiram treatment in the chapter by D. Raistrick on 'Helping Those Who Want To Change'. "It is often useful to give a test dose of alcohol (say the equivalent of two pints of beer) to clients taking disulfiram to confirm to them the disulfiram–ethanol reaction. (This alcohol challenge is not intended to produce an unduly unpleasant effect). It is important to achieve an effective dose level because clients will often test out whether or not they can drink on top of disulfiram . . . the results of disulfiram therapy are impressive." There is an adequate description of the work of Azrin *et al*, with references. "The programme is abstinence orientated and participants all receive Antabuse taken under carefully prepared conditions supervised by their spouse or a significant other. . . . At six month follow up clients receiving [unsupervised] disulfiram and supportive counselling reported over 50% drinking days compared to virtually no drinking for individuals in community reinforcement, who also did better in terms of employment and time spent at home.''

Drinking Problems (Chick & Chick, 1992)

There are two index references to Antabuse and one to calcium carbimide. Strictly speaking, this is not a textbook, being more designed for alcohol abusers and/or their families. However, although lacking references, it includes an excellent summary of the importance and techniques of supervision and of the rationale of treatment. ''These medicines help establish a period of stability in which to get life reorganised. Injured self-esteem has a chance to recover.'' Medication should be supervised by ''your partner or someone at work''. It was the only book to describe the common evasion techniques and how to circumvent them. ''Put the tablet into water so that it breaks up and then you cannot hide it under your tongue and pretend you have swallowed it. Your supervisor can also check that you have not substituted aspirins because Antabuse and Abstem tablets are marked.''

Managing Alcoholism: Matching Clients to Treatments (Lindstrom, 1992)

There are eight index references to disulfiram, and three to calcium carbimide. In a chapter entitled 'The Social Model', there is an exhaustive description of Azrin's work, covering some 23 pages, thoroughly referenced. Lindstrom notes that despite its documented effectiveness, CRT is not widely used or discussed. He describes the use of disulfiram (and calcium carbimide) in prevention of relapse and mentions that ''it gives the help-seeker an opportunity to experience success . . . in a large number of ways. The daily Antabuse ritual, for example, verifies in symbolic form the alcohol-dependent person's victory over his craving for alcohol. This seems to be an effective method for certain persons, at least as long as other significant people convince them of the meaningfulness of their endeavours.''

Alcoholism Treatment: Process and Outcome (Moos et al, 1990)

There are three index entries. It contains a thorough review of Azrin's work, including the finding that married patients generally did well with supervised disulfiram alone. ''Taken as a whole, our findings show that more intensive participation and psychological treatment and the use of Antabuse are related to better outcome.''

Discussion

Given the effectiveness of supervised disulfiram, it is worrying that the majority of these textbooks either do not discuss disulfiram treatment in any detail (or at all, in some cases) or else discuss it without reference to any of the relevant research. Only eight indicated that supervision was important, but five of these did not mention any of the relevant studies. The authors who are lukewarm or dismissive about disulfiram do not appear to base their conclusions on a review of the literature. In contrast, those who are more enthusiastic generally cite controlled trials, while the most persuasive authors are those who have evidently read and digested the literature. They are also less inclined to be alarmist about the risks of disulfiram, although they may give more weight to the high mortality of unchecked alcohol abuse.

It is perhaps less surprising that social workers like Collins or psychologists like Saunders appear reluctant to describe the effectiveness of a medical treatment. However, it is puzzling that academic authors who have no obvious ideological or professional objection to the use of disulfiram mention none of the relevant research findings.

Most authors state or imply that disulfiram should be used only when abstinence is the goal of treatment. This ignores the evidence that many patients attempting controlled drinking use disulfiram or calcium carbimide to help them to abstain for short periods, if they feel their drinking is getting out of control, or to prevent them from drinking in specific high-risk situations (Duckert & Johnson, 1986).

With disulfiram, as with all drugs, adequate dosage is important. Although Peachey states baldly that "The therapeutic dose of it is 250 mg daily", most of the authors who discuss disulfiram mention that the dose may need to be increased if the reaction with alcohol is too mild to deter drinking, or suggest a dose range between 250 and 500 mg daily (see p. 41). This contrasts with the recommended maximum in the British manufacturer's data sheet of 200 mg daily. Several authors claim that disulfiram has a slow onset of action or that it is "slowly absorbed" (Edwards, 1987). This is probably incorrect. Several patients have told me that they took disulfiram to try to abort a drinking bout and experienced a reaction within an hour. Disulfiram certainly causes prolonged inhibition of acetaldehyde metabolism, but no author mentions that in consequence, administration of the drug – and supervision – can often be reduced to thrice or twice weekly.

Arguably, a textbook about alcoholism treatment or prevention of relapse that does not discuss supervised disulfiram in detail is as defective as one about respiratory disease that fails to discuss antibiotics or artificial ventilation. It has been said that it takes ten years for a new treatment to get into the textbooks – and another ten years to get it out of them when it has proved to be ineffective. The evidence for the effectiveness of supervised disulfiram has been accumulating steadily since 1967, with no contrary findings. After 26 years, it has surely earned a more established place in our therapeutic repertoire than this review indicates.

References

ANDERSON, P., WALLACE, P. & JONES, H. (1989) *Alcohol Problems (Practical Guides for General Practice No. 5)*. Oxford: Oxford University Press.
AZRIN, N. H., SISSON, R. W., MEYERS, R., *et al* (1982) Alcoholism treatment by disulfiram and community reinforcement therapy. *Journal of Behaviour Therapy and Experimental Psychiatry*, **13**, 105–112.
BREWER, C. (1987) Fact, fiction, finance and effectiveness in alcoholism treatment. *British Journal of Clinical Practice*, **41**, 39–46.
—— (1992) Controlled trials of Antabuse in alcoholism: the importance of supervision and adequate dosage. *Acta Psychiatrica Scandinavica*, **86**, 51–58.
CHICK, J. & CHICK, J. (1992) *Drinking Problems*. London: Optima.
——, GOUGH, K., WOJCIECH, F., *et al* (1992) Disulfiram treatment of alcoholism. *British Journal of Psychiatry*, **161**, 84–89.
CIRAULO, D. A. & SHADER, R. I. (1990) *A Manual for Chemical Dependence*. Washington, DC: American Psychiatric Press.
COLLINS, S. (ed.) (1990) *Alcohol, Social Work and Helping*. London: Routledge.
DAVIDSON, R., ROLLNICK, S. & McEWAN, I. (eds) (1991) *Counselling Problem Drinkers*. London: Routledge.
DUCKERT, F. & JOHNSEN, J. (1986) Behavioural use of disulfiram in the treatment of problem drinking. *International Journal of Addiction*, **22**, 445–454.
EDWARDS, G. (1987) *The Treatment of Drinking Problems: A Guide for the Helping Professions* (2nd edn). Oxford: Blackwell.
FRANCES, R. J. & FRANKLIN, J. E. (1989) *Concise Guide to Treatment of Alcoholism and Addictions*. Washington, DC: American Psychiatric Press.
GALLANT, D. M. (1987) *Alcoholism, A Guide to Diagnosis, Intervention and Treatment*. New York: Norton.
GERREIN, J., ROSENBERY, C. & MANOHAR, V. (1973) Disulfiram maintenance in outpatient treatment of alcoholism. *Archives of General Psychiatry*, **28**, 798–802.
GHODSE, H. (1989) *Drugs and Addictive Behaviour: A Guide to Treatment*. Oxford: Blackwell.
GLASS, I. B. (ed.) (1991) *The International Handbook of Addiction Behaviour*. London: Tavistock.
GOSSOP, M. (1989) *Relapse and Addictive Behaviour*. London: Routledge.
HEATHER, N. & ROBERTSON, I. (1990) *Controlled Drinking* (2nd edn). Oxford: Oxford Medical.
LIEBSON, I., BIGELOW, G. & FLAMER, R. (1973) Alcoholism among methadone patients, a specific treatment method. *American Journal of Psychiatry*, **130**, 483–485.
LINDSTROM, L. (1992) *Managing Alcoholism: Matching Clients to Treatment*. Oxford: Oxford Medical.
LITTRELL, J. (1991) *Understanding and Treating Alcoholism*, Vol. 2. Hillsdale: Lawrence.
MILLER, N. S. (ed.) (1991) *Comprehensive Handbook of Drug and Alcohol Addiction*. New York: Decker.
MILLER, W. (1989) The effectiveness of alcoholism treatment modalities: causes and consequences of alcohol abuse. *Hearings before the Committee on Government Affairs Part III: US Senate*, 171–185.
MOOS, R. H., FINNEY, J. W. & CRONKITE, R. C. (1990) *Alcoholism Treatment: Process and Outcome*. Oxford: Oxford University Press.
SAUNDERS, B. (1985) Treatment does not work: some criteria of failure. In *The Misuse of Alcohol: Crucial Issues in Dependence, Treatment & Prevention* (eds N. Heather, I. Robertson & P. Davies), pp. 112–116. London: Croom Helm.
SERENY, G., SHARMA, V., HOLT, J., *et al* (1986) Mandatory supervised Antabuse therapy in an outpatient alcoholism program: a pilot study. *Alcoholism: Clinical and Experimental Research*, **10**, 290–292.
WANIGARATNE, S., WALLACE, W., PULLEN, J., *et al* (1990) *Relapse Prevention for Addictive Behaviours, A Manual for Therapists*. Oxford: Blackwell.

4 Probation-linked treatment with disulfiram: dosage and the alcohol–disulfiram challenge

COLIN BREWER

Despite the fact that prisons are generally unpleasant, dilapidated, degrading, and dangerous places, offenders are not necessarily deterred by their experiences of incarceration, and recidivism is common. It has been said that prisons deter those who walk past their doors, but not those who walk through them. As well as having all these disadvantages, prisons are also expensive to run. Therefore, anything which helps to keep offenders out of prison without posing unacceptable risks of re-offending is desirable on both humane and economic grounds. And since "It is impossible to train men for freedom in a condition of captivity" (Paterson, 1932), this is also desirable on therapeutic grounds, because prisons are generally unsuitable places for treatment.

Recurrent alcoholic offenders are often difficult therapeutic subjects: a higher proportion of them than of general alcoholic patients are isolated, rather marginal in society, and unskilled. They also have a high propensity for taking risks, and some of them are brain-damaged. Nevertheless, the surprising thing about research into the use of probation-linked disulfiram is that the results of treatment are fairly good. However, in view of the evidence of its efficacy presented elsewhere in this volume, perhaps it is not so surprising that if they can be persuaded to take disulfiram, then even marginal, unskilled, isolated, and brain-damaged alcoholics will generally stop drinking.

If people with serious, recurrent drinking problems are offered the possibility of taking disulfiram and some firm advice to do so, many of them will take it up. Sereny *et al* (1986) studied a group of patients who had had three relapses despite treatment in a good, conventional, abstinence-based programme. Eventually, these patients were told that the authors would like to help, but that nothing they did had seemed to do much good; therefore, they were only prepared to offer further treatment to those who would come to the clinic three times a week and take disulfiram under supervision. Out of 73 patients, 68 accepted these conditions. Their criteria for success and failure were fairly stringent, as shown below.

TABLE 4.1
Treatment outcome of patients on supervised mandatory disulfiram

Outcome	No. (%) of patients
Total success	27 (40)
Partial success	12 (18)
Failure	20 (29)
Undetermined	9 (13)

Source: Sereny *et al*, 1986

(a) Total success
    (i) Sober for at least six months and remains in the mandatory disulfiram programme at the time of the study
      or
    (ii) Discharged from mandatory disulfiram after 12 months of sobriety.

(b) Partial success
    (i) Patient had three to six months of sobriety on mandatory disulfiram at the time of the study
      or
    (ii) Patient remained sober on mandatory disulfiram for more than six months, but then drank.

(c) Failure
    Drank or missed two appointments within three months of joining the mandatory disulfiram programme.

(d) Undetermined
    Sober on mandatory disulfiram for less than three months.

Table 4.1 shows the results in a group of patients who would normally be regarded as having a poor prognosis: almost 60% were either successful or partly successful, which must be considered a good outcome, even when compared with a group of relatively stable, married patients presenting for treatment for the first time (Edwards *et al*, 1977). Although the patients of Sereny *et al* were not defined by their offending status, many of them would probably have experienced at least short-term imprisonment for alcohol-related behaviour. It is largely matters of chance, geography, physiology, economics, and personality which decide whether a recurrent alcoholic becomes a recurrent alcoholic *offender*, a recurrent alcoholic *patient*, or an alcoholic death.

Studies of probation-linked disulfiram

The first report of the use of probation-linked disulfiram was by Bourne *et al* (1966). In the USA, much more than in the UK, there is a tendency to give recurrent alcoholic offenders 30–90 days in jail without an option. The patients in this study were given an option – that of supervised disulfiram – and over half of them took it regularly for at least three months. Several had served as much as ten years in jail in consecutive sentences, but after starting disulfiram, they remained abstinent for several months and some were able to hold steady jobs. That is very similar to what Brahen (see p. 48) has reported about some of his naltrexone-treated patients.

Some of these offender-patients, like the ordinary patients of Azrin *et al* (1982) who needed little but supervised disulfiram to do well, also did not need much apart from properly supervised disulfiram, despite their very unpromising histories. This was not a controlled trial, but its considered conclusion was that the combination of disulfiram with the authority of the court can be very helpful in the treatment of some alcoholic offenders.

More impressive is a study of probation-linked disulfiram carried out in Colorado Springs by Haynes (1973) involving 141 patients, three of whom actually said that they would prefer to go to prison for three months and drink when they came out. The others accepted the alternative of 12 months on supervised disulfiram. Again, about half of them took it regularly, with the spectacular results mentioned on p. 6 by Heather. This massive reduction, of about 12- or 13-fold, in the re-arrest rate for alcoholic offences is one of the major therapeutic achievements in the whole of criminological research. Yet this paper is very little known and hardly ever mentioned, despite being published in the *Journal of Behavior Therapy and Experimental Psychiatry*.

This treatment programme has been going for over 25 years and is still strongly favoured by judges, probation officers, and the police. Colorado Springs is not a town with a large 'skid-row' population, but is an agreeable place at the foot of the Rocky Mountains with half a million inhabitants. It is evidently well known there that if an offender fails to turn up twice a week and take his disulfiram, there will very quickly be a police car on the doorstep. Probationers are not automatically imprisoned if they are not taking disulfiram as agreed, but they get a strong warning and a reminder of the terms of the probation order. This is surely one of the functions of probation work.

Brewer & Smith (1983) published a pilot study of 16 habitual drunken offenders in London who had an average of 6.3 alcohol-related convictions and an average maximum period of abstinence outside prison of only six weeks. They were offered regular counselling and supervised disulfiram as conditions of probation. Not all of them would have expected a further prison sentence for the current offence, but many would, and only one refused the offer. At the end of the study, the average maximum period of abstinence for the whole group was 30 weeks, and all but one of them had exceeded their longest abstinence in the previous two years. The one exception was rather unusual, because he had had some quite long periods of abstinence in the past.

This too was not a controlled trial, but the results were very encouraging and in line with similar studies previously discussed.

Dosage of disulfiram

If patients are to take disulfiram, it is important that they have enough; as with all drugs, not everyone responds to the same dose. The standard dose recommended in the UK is 200 mg daily, but that is insufficient for a significant proportion of patients. In the USA, the recommended doses are 250–500 mg daily. A retrospective study (Brewer, 1984) found that about 50% of patients do not get much reaction with alcohol on doses of between 200 mg and 300 mg of disulfiram daily. This proportion decreased sharply as the dose of disulfiram is increased, but one patient failed to react even on a dose of 1.2 g daily. In a prospective study using volunteers (Christensen *et al*, 1991), only a minority of those taking up to 300 mg daily experienced a reaction after 10 g of alcohol which was thought to be unpleasant enough to make them refuse a second drink.

Disulfiram was introduced into clinical practice over 40 years ago and this may explain why its pharmacokinetics have not, until recently, received much study using sophisticated biochemical methods. It now appears that disulfiram may be a pro-drug which has to be metabolised to another compound, diethylthiocarbamic acid methyl ester, before the enzyme inhibition which causes the reaction with alcohol *in vivo* can take place (Johansson *et al*, 1991; Kitson, 1991; Petersen, 1992). This biotransformation may well involve the liver; severe liver disease or individual metabolic idiosyncrasies may sometimes reduce or prevent the formation of the active metabolite of disulfiram (Johansson & Stankiewicz, 1989). Different formulations of disulfiram may also have very different bioavailabilities and as with many other drugs, absorption may be modified by food (Andersen, 1992). This means that achieving adequate dosage is not always straightforward and that an alcohol challenge is still sometimes necessary.

The alcohol challenge

A challenge may be appropriate in cases where it would be particularly undesirable for the patient to risk drinking alcohol, only to find that there was little or no reaction; for example, where patients who have one more drunken episode in the next year will go to prison, lose their job, or find themselves without spouse or home.

The disulfiram–ethanol reaction (DER) on having a challenge dose of alcohol can occur after only a single measure (25 ml) of 40% spirits. In carrying out an alcohol challenge, there is usually no need to go beyond that point, since it has been established that the patient gets a significant reaction to even a small dose of alcohol. Most patients will accept that if they were to take a larger dose of alcohol, they would get a more unpleasant reaction. Most patients do not need to experience the DER because they either believe it when they are told they will get a reaction if they drink alcohol, or they have friends who drank on disulfiram and became very ill. They may still be deterred even if they also know of people who risked drinking alcohol and did *not* get much of a reaction.

The traditional technique for giving an alcohol challenge was described in earlier versions of the manufacturer's data sheet. Four tablets (800 mg) of disulfiram are given on the first day, reducing by one tablet each subsequent day to a maintenance dose of 200 mg daily. On the fifth day, the patient is given a challenge dose containing 15–30 g of pure ethanol. However, disulfiram is slowly excreted at a variable rate, and it seems unlikely that blood levels will have stabilised so soon after a succession of changing daily doses. The result of this test may therefore be misleading. Furthermore, 15 g of ethanol may be more than enough in some patients to produce a very unpleasant reaction. The usual object of the challenge dose is not to make the patient feel ill, but merely to convince him that something unpleasant will indeed happen if he drinks significant amounts of alcohol and that the whole procedure is not, as some patients appear to suspect, a rather ingenious bluff.

There is a kinder and less hazardous alternative. The challenge is not done until patients have been on a consistent dose of disulfiram for at least five days. The initial dose of alcohol consists of only 12 ml of 40% spirits (about 5 g ethanol) on an empty stomach. A few patients produce a definite flush on that dosage, in which case they need no further alcohol, but most do not and if there is no reaction after 20 minutes, they receive a further 25 ml of spirits (approx. 10 g ethanol) or a little more if they are heavier than average. At this dosage of alcohol, a positive result rarely consists of anything more than a noticeable flushing with tachycardia and sometimes a slight fall in blood pressure. If there is no reaction, the dosage of disulfiram is increased and the test repeated after an interval of at least a week, until a positive result is obtained. The alcohol challenge is done as an out-patient procedure (Brewer, 1984).

Despite a positive challenge, some patients risk drinking while taking disulfiram and discover that the reaction is not severe enough to stop them in their tracks, but if that happens, the dose should be increased until drinking stops or side-effects become a problem. Given the impulsive nature of many alcoholic offenders, such testing-out is hardly surprising. The impulsivity is not simply a question of personality. Some are impulsive at least in part because of brain damage due to alcohol and/or repeated head injuries, and they may have lost a considerable amount of brain tissue

(Brewer & Perrett, 1971; Ron *et al*, 1980). This factor is of clinical and practical importance in chronic alcoholic patients.

Toxicity, side-effects and drug interactions

As indicated in the review of attitudes to disulfiram in various textbooks (Chapter 3), attitudes to its side-effects vary considerably. A recent review (Poulson *et al*, 1992) analyses spontaneous reports of adverse drug reactions (ADR) to disulfiram to the Danish Committee on ADRs from 1968 to 1991, as well as reports to the WHO Centre for International Drug Monitoring. Their conclusions are that disulfiram has an 'intermediate' incidence of ADRs (1/200–1/2000 per treatment year) and that the risk of death from the only potentially lethal side-effect, disulfiram hepatitis, is one in 25 000 patients per year. A disproportionate number of hepatitis cases involved patients treated not for alcoholism but for nickel or cobalt allergy. Disulfiram neuropathy is generally associated with prolonged treatment and/or higher doses, and is usually reversible if the drug is discontinued or the dosage reduced. Drowsiness is the commonest side-effect reported in most studies; it usually diminishes after a few days and may be associated with the higher loading doses traditionally recommended. Patients who need a deterrent drug but who do not tolerate disulfiram well may be treated with calcium carbimide, but disulfiram is to be preferred because its much longer duration of action makes supervision of administration much easier.

Larson *et al* (1992) conclude that "At the usual dosage, about 250 mg/day, disulfiram does not appear to increase significantly the risk of psychiatric complications or of psychiatric drug interactions [and] can be considered a treatment option for patients with alcohol dependence and other psychiatric disorders". The risk of death following deliberate overdosage is low, especially in comparison with drugs such as tricyclic antidepressants. Even if disulfiram had a much higher incidence of serious side-effects, this would have to be set against the much greater toxicity of alcohol and the mortality rates of 10–20% reported in many long-term follow-up studies of alcohol abuse (Vaillant, 1973; Edwards *et al*, 1983).

Ethical and practical issues

Although these issues are crucial, there is much misunderstanding about them. Nobody can force a patient on probation or facing imprisonment to take disulfiram. However, what can be said to him is, in effect, that he seems to be going in and out of prison and that at the present rate, this is likely to continue, so that it would surely be much better if he would agree, as a condition of probation, to take disulfiram so that he can maximise his chances of staying sober and thus remain in treatment for long enough to be rehabilitated. If he should change his mind, however, that is his own choice: a probation order is an agreement which a patient enters into, and he can alter this at any stage. In fact, many patients welcome treatment in a firm, contractual framework, as the study by Sereny *et al* (1986), mentioned above, showed. The view of the General Medical Council is that there is no ethical objection, provided that the patient has been adequately informed of the nature and risks of treatment.

Supervised disulfiram, particularly if it is supervised by the probation service, as it should be and as it is in Colorado Springs, has some of the advantages of methadone maintenance. The patient has to go regularly to take the medication, and that has both symbolic value – somebody cares enough about him to give him his medication – and practical value. If the offender goes to a place regularly, even if it is only for five minutes a day, he or she has a contact point where there is no need to make an excuse to go along and talk about a problem. If they have to go to the probation office anyway, it is quite easy to get in touch with their probation officer and maybe deal with the problem before it gets out of hand.

References

ANDERSEN, M. P. (1992) Lack of bioequivalence between disulfiram formulations, exemplified by a tablet/effervescent tablet study. *Acta Psychiatrica Scandinavica*, **86**, 31–35.

AZRIN, N. H., SISSONS, R. W., MAYER, S. R., *et al* (1982) Alcoholism treatment by disulfiram and community reinforcement therapy. *Journal of Behavior Therapy and Experimental Psychiatry*, **13**, 105–112.

BOURNE, P. G., ALFORD, J. A. & BOWCOCK, J. Z. (1966) Treatment of skid row alcoholics with disulfiram. *Quarterly Journal of Studies on Alcohol*, **27**, 42–48.

BREWER, C. (1984) How effective is the standard dose of disulfiram? A review of the disulfiram-alcohol reaction in practice. *British Journal of Psychiatry*, **144**, 200–202.

—— & PERRETT, L. (1971) Brain damage due to alcohol consumption: a psychometric, air-encephalographic and EEG study. *British Journal of Addiction*, **66**, 170–182.

—— & SMITH, J. (1983) Probation-linked supervised disulfiram in the treatment of habitual drunken offenders: results of a pilot study. *British Medical Journal*, **287**, 1282–1283.

CHRISTENSEN, J. K., MELLER, I. W., IRONSTED, P., *et al* (1991) Dose-effect relationship of disulfiram in human volunteers. I: Clinical studies. *Pharmacology and Toxicology*, **68**, 163–165.

EDWARDS, G., ORFORD, J. & EGERT, S. (1977) Alcoholism: a controlled trial of 'treatment' and 'advice'. *Quarterly Journal of Studies of Alcohol*, **38**, 1004–1033.

——, DUCKITT, A., OPPENHEIMER, E., *et al* (1983) What happens to alcoholics? *Lancet*, **ii**, 269–271.

HAYNES, S. N. (1973) Contingency management in a municipally administered Antabuse program for alcoholics. *Journal of Behaviour Therapy and Experimental Psychiatry*, **4**, 31–32.

JOHANSSON, B. & STANKIEWICZ, Z. (1989) Inhibition of erythrocyte aldehyde dehydrogenase activity and elimination kinetics of diethyldithiocarbamic acid methyl ester and its monothio analogue after administration of single and repeated doses of disulfiram to man. *European Journal of Clinical Pharmacology*, **37**, 133–138.

——, ANGELO, H., CHRISTENSEN, J., *et al* (1991) Dose-effect relationship of disulfiram in human volunteers II: A study of the relationship between the disulfiram-alcohol reaction and plasma concentrations of acetaldehyde, diethyldithiocarbamic acid methyl ester and erythrocyte aldehyde dehydrogenase activity. *Pharmacology and Toxicology*, **68**, 166–170.

KITSON, T. (1991) Effect of some thiocarbamate compounds on aldehyde dehydrogenase and implications for the disulfiram ethanol reaction. *Biochemical Journal*, **278**, 189–192.

LARSON, E. W., OLINCY, A., RUMMANS, T. A., *et al* (1992) Disulfiram treatment of patients with both alcohol dependence and other psychiatric disorders: a review. *Alcoholism: Clinical and Experimental Research*, **16**, 125–130.

PATERSON, A. (1932) *Principles of the Borstal System*. London: London Prison Commission.

PETERSEN, E. N. (1992) The pharmacology and toxicology of disulfiram and its metabolites. *Acta Psychiatrica Scandinavica*, **86**, 7–13.

POULSEN, H. E., LOFT, S., ANDERSEN, J. R., *et al* (1992) Disulfiram therapy – adverse drug reactions and interactions. *Acta Psychiatrica Scandinavica*, **86**, 59–66.

RON, M. A., ACKER, W. & LISHMAN, W. A. (1980) Morphological abnormalities in the brains of chronic alcoholics: a clinical psychological and computerized axial tomographical study. *Acta Psychiatrica Scandinavica* (suppl. 286), 41–46.

SERENY, G., SHARMA, V., HOLT, J., *et al* (1986) Mandatory supervised Antabuse therapy in an out-patient alcoholism program: a pilot study. *Alcoholism: Clinical and Experimental Research*, **10**, 290–292.

VAILLANT, G. E. (1973) A twenty-year follow-up of New York narcotic addicts. *Archives of General Psychiatry*, **29**, 237–241.

5 Naltrexone in the criminal justice system

LEONARD S. BRAHEN and COLIN BREWER

Since 1972, selected non-violent prisoners have been allowed out of Nassau County Jail during the day to work or to attend training courses. Because of the poor image of heroin addicts and the obviously high risk that relapse during work release will lead to further criminal activity, prisoners with a history of opiate abuse were initially not allowed to apply for the programme, even if they fulfilled all other criteria for acceptance. It therefore seemed important to find ways of making such prisoners eligible for work release, without unacceptable risks to the community. In 1972, the Nassau County Department of Drug & Alcohol Addiction, in cooperation with the Nassau County Jail, initiated the Narcotic Antagonist Jail Work Release Program (Brahen *et al*, 1974), using the opioid antagonist naltrexone (the mode of action and general use of which are discussed in Chapter 6).

Selection

For the work-release programme, candidates were sought who were motivated to become drug-free, productive citizens, and who hoped that naltrexone would help to strengthen their resolve (Capone & Brahen, 1980; National Institute on Drug Abuse, 1980). All candidates for the programme, whether or not they have a history of opiate abuse, must submit a written request for work release. An exhaustive review is made, including of the drug and criminal history, and the findings are presented to the Institutional Review Board for approval. In the case of addicted offenders, members of the Narcotic Antagonist Treatment Team serve as consultants, but have no vote. The age-limits are 18 to 45. Fertile women are eligible if they use oral contraceptives or are fitted with an intrauterine device. All studies to date have been approved by the Institutional Review Board, the Federal Drug Administration, the National Institute on Drug Abuse, and the National Institute for Protection of Human Rights. In addition, the informed consent protocol is read to each entrant by a nurse or doctor and is signed by all parties (Brahen *et al*, 1977a).

Patients entering the programme have a complete medical examination, a chest X-ray, urine analysis, and a battery of laboratory tests. These are repeated yearly, and more frequently if necessary (Brahen *et al*, 1977*b*).

Naltrexone administration

Before starting treatment with naltrexone, a minimum opioid-free period of seven days is required in the case of methadone and of three days for heroin. The initial dose is 12.5 mg of naltrexone (a quarter of a tablet), and the patient is observed closely for half an hour. If no withdrawal symptoms are observed, full doses are then given.

Dosage schedules

One 50 mg tablet provides at least 24 hours of opioid blockade, and this can be extended with higher doses. The following schedules are in use:

(a) 50 mg daily
(b) 100 mg on Monday and Wednesday, 150 mg on Friday
(c) 150 mg on Monday, 200 mg on Thursday

The twice-weekly schedule produces effective opioid blockade with freedom from major side-effects, and is the one most frequently used.

Precipitated opiate withdrawal

Occasionally, patients give an inaccurate drug-taking history, and naltrexone may then cause a precipitated abstinence syndrome. When this occurs, patients are placed under constant monitoring and vital signs are checked frequently. If indicated, the doctor will prescribe medication for nausea or vomiting, as well as sedatives – preferably non-benzodiazepines – for anxiety and insomnia. Such events are most likely to occur in out-patients and in those who remain in treatment after their final release from prison; in our experience, no patient of this kind has required in-patient treatment.

Side-effects

Other than precipitated withdrawal, naltrexone has been free of major untoward effects; in controlled studies, it has been found to have no more side-effects than placebo (Brahen *et al*, 1988), although gastrointestinal symptoms have been reported in other studies. Because this population of prisoners was generally free of all illicit drugs for at least one month before entering the programme, many longer-term opioid withdrawal symptoms may have been eliminated (Brahen *et al*, 1977*a*).

Monitoring during the programme

The prisoner's health, behaviour, and illicit drug use are monitored; urine samples are collected randomly on returning from work to the prison. The first three or four infractions, such as positive urine samples, are handled through a penalty-point system. Alcohol breathalyser tests are also administered. Repeated infractions may lead to removal from the minimum security work-release environment to the higher security main jail, while lesser penalties include loss of weekend leave (Brahen *et al*, 1973).

Support services

To maximise the potential for successful re-entry into the community after the jail sentence is served, strong support services are provided by the treatment team. Each inmate has an appointment with an individual professional counsellor on one evening each week. Since alcohol and polydrug abuse is frequently noted, the implications of dependence and possible treatment strategies are discussed.

Also, a vocational rehabilitation counsellor assesses the strengths and work potential of each patient. Participants in the programme complete both vocational-interest inventory-preference schedules and aptitude tests. Suitably qualified inmates may receive financial support for training through the New York State Office of Vocational Rehabilitation.

Before re-entry into the community, social workers make appropriate referrals and community contacts. Attempts are made to help with financial matters, employment, family relationships, legal advice, and appropriate treatment (Kleber, 1973). Patients also have the option of post-release treatment at the adjoining Nassau County Medical Center. Of over a thousand people treated with naltrexone, approximately one-third were involved in the jail programme.

Benefits of the programme

Many day-release participants found that for the first time in their lives, they could hold down a job (Capone & Brahen, 1980). They also learned to respect the capacity of naltrexone to block opioid effects. The treatment team found that the behaviour problems of those taking naltrexone were no different from the problems of prisoners in the work-release programme who had no history of opioid abuse. The attrition rates for the two groups were comparable, at around 25%. Compared with pre-incarceration drug-related arrests of addicted offenders, the narcotic antagonist group had significantly fewer such arrests after release, although the groups were not randomised (Brahen *et al*, 1984).

A study has been carried out by Tilly *et al* (1991) of the University of Pennsylvania Center for studies on Addiction, in collaboration with the local probation service. Sixty-three probationers convicted of opiate-related offences were randomly allocated to twice-weekly probation counselling, with and without supervised naltrexone; 48% of this group took naltrexone regularly for at least six months. The results show a significant reduction in subsequent incarceration for the naltrexone group.

Such programmes therefore provide opportunities for work or training for non-violent prisoners who have a history of opiate abuse. Although they constitute a majority of the prisoners in Nassau County Jail, their history would have precluded these possibilities, but for naltrexone. Finally, the opiate-addicted inmate in this programme has achieved a highly important change of status. Before the narcotic-antagonist programme, the addict was considered to be at high risk and was relegated to the bottom of the 'trust ladder' (Brahen *et al*, 1984). The prison administration now views naltrexone-programme participants as among the most trustworthy in the facility. This was demonstrated in 1986, when a weekend-leave programme was started, and most of the original participants were selected from the narcotic-antagonist population.

Part of the work-release participants' salary is set aside to assist their re-entry into the community; they also pay a contribution to the jail for board and lodging. This provides inmates with a sense of accomplishment and importance that welfare programmes cannot duplicate. So far, over 200 released prisoners have continued with naltrexone treatment after release. Others have remained in out-patient treatment, with urine monitoring and counselling but without naltrexone. As well as being non-addictive, naltrexone has no street value and therefore does not enter into illicit channels (Jasinski *et al*, 1973).

The Narcotic Antagonist Jail Work Release Program appears to have a role in the rehabilitation of addicted offenders (Ginzburg & MacDonald, 1987). At a time when jails cannot be built fast enough to house the influx of convicted heroin addicts, an alternative treatment programme which could also save the taxpayer up to 90% of the costs of incarceration should perhaps be considered. In this programme, consenting non-violent drug offenders would be referred to the probation-parole system, which would then take overall responsibility for the convicted addict, referring him to an out-patient naltrexone-treatment programme.

The naltrexone programme should have rigid requirements regarding supervised urine testing, work, and attendance at the clinic, as well as an agreement that the therapist-counsellor can immediately report all infractions and problems. Decisions to terminate treatment should be made by the probation or parole officer, in cooperation with the counsellor. Trust and respect must be established between probation or parole officers and the treatment team, and methods for assessing effectiveness must also be built into any new approach.

Probation-linked naltrexone

Nobody in the UK has treated large numbers of offenders with naltrexone in court-mandated programmes comparable to those described by Brahen above or by Tilly *et al* (1991). However, the most satisfactory arrangement has been when offenders were released from prison on bail with a condition that they resided at a bail hostel where the staff were willing to administer naltrexone under supervision. Pre-trial compliance has been generally good, but the hostel cannot usually accommodate offenders once they are on probation, so post-trial compliance has often lapsed because of poor supervision. However, several failed naltrexone patients have successfully transferred to oral or intravenous methadone programmes, with monitoring for illicit drug use. The study of probation-linked naltrexone by Tilly *et al* (1991) has confirmed the specific value of oral naltrexone in reducing heroin-related crime, as well as the importance of an adequate dose and of careful supervision. The availability of a depot injection of naltrexone, currently undergoing clinical trials, should greatly reduce problems of compliance.

An impression that the courts favour this approach to drug-related offenders has subsequently been confirmed by a survey of London magistrates (Johns & Gossop, 1990). Most courts in the UK seem anxious to avoid imprisoning the sort of people they tend to define as 'sick' rather than 'wicked'; in that sense, their definition merits support. Therefore, the courts are often very interested in incorporating into a probation order treatments like disulfiram, naltrexone, or methadone maintenance (even intravenous methadone) that are targeted on the behaviour which is particularly likely to lead to further offences.

At the same time, just as the courts usually like to have more than the mere assurance of the offender – however sincere – that he will obey the law in future, they also like to have, if possible, more than just a promise that offenders will take their medication as prescribed. They like to know that someone will monitor them and that urine, breath, or liver-function tests will be done. Hair analysis for illicit drugs (Chapter 12) is a new and useful addition to monitoring techniques which is often attractive to the courts.

Ideological objections to probation-linked treatment

Hostility to probation-linked treatments comes mainly from the probation officers themselves and also from pressure groups like Out of Court and the National Association for the Care & Resettlement of Offenders (NACRO), although these might be expected to favour alternatives to prison. The National Association of Probation Officers (NAPO) is rather opposed to attaching conditions to probation orders.

Another problem is that the staff of probation and social services include many who adhere to Freudian doctrines; they disapprove of naltrexone and disulfiram because they feel that these drugs do not do anything about the underlying emotional problems which, the doctrines tell them, are at the root of all addictions. This is not a well founded idea. Of course, many offenders have enormous problems, but these are often the *result* of their addiction and not a cause: if they can be kept dry or 'clean' for some time, many of the problems will diminish or disappear. They will certainly be much more likely then to respond to interventions aimed at those problems which are not a direct consequence of their addiction. Fortunately, this opposition seems to be diminishing. In part, this may be because the threat of privatisation or contracting out which hangs over the probation service has concentrated minds on questions of effectiveness rather than professional politics. (Opposition to methadone maintenance programmes based on a belief that 'drug free' treatment is the only acceptable modality is a separate issue and is discussed elsewhere in this volume.)

Further studies are certainly needed in this numerically important and ethically contentious field. The results of US studies involving disulfiram and naltrexone are encouraging, but it might be unwise to assume that an approach which works within one particular legal system can be transferred unchanged to other and perhaps very different jurisdictions. It would be difficult to have a classical, randomised, double-blind controlled trial of these regimes, but matched controls are clearly possible and precedents exist in the UK for studies involving randomised sentencing. In Edinburgh, Hamilton (1979) managed to arrange for public drunkenness offenders to be randomised to a detoxification centre or to the usual night or two in the police cells. He found that those placed in the police cells subsequently drank less than those referred to the centre, although the difference was not statistically significant. In the Leeds Truancy Study (Berg *et al*, 1978), truants were randomly sentenced to two very different approaches, and the results showed that traditional social work was significantly less effective than simpler techniques based on the authority of the court.

The concept of probation-linked treatment seems to have little potential for harm. On the other hand, it has a considerable potential for good. Like all treatments, it will not help everyone, but no treatment for offenders can be expected to be either perfect or permanent. If someone would normally have gone to prison for a year because the judge felt that he had to protect the public against that offender's alcohol- or heroin-related crime, the judge might be persuaded that there was a reasonable chance of keeping that person free of alcohol or heroin for a year on probation-linked disulfiram or naltrexone. The offender might relapse at the end of the probation order, but the same applies when he comes out of prison. Improvement does not have to be permanent, but if someone gets used to living in the community for a year without alcohol or heroin, there is surely a better chance that he will continue to abstain, even when the probation order has expired.

Naltrexone has a negligible incidence of significant side-effects, but it should always be remembered that even if the incidence were substantial, the mortality from heroin abuse in many follow-up studies, particularly for this kind of offender, is 10–20% (Tunving, 1988). To be over-concerned about the small risks of treatment in this situation suggests a rather unrealistic set of priorities.

Acknowledgements

LSB thanks Commissioner Harold E. Adams, ACSW, Deputy Commissioner Raymond J. Condren, PhD; Myrtle Peterson, ACSW, Director of Drug Treatment Services, Eugene Thompson, MD, Medical Director, Methadone Treatment Program, and Ronald Melchionda, CSW, Director Substance Alternative Clinic for their helpful comments and suggestions; and Eleanor Lisa and Carol Germano for editorial assistance.

References

BERG, I., CONSTERDINE, M., HULLIN, R., et al (1978) The effect of two randomly allocated court procedures on truancy. *British Journal of Criminology*, **18**, 232–244.

BRAHEN, L. S., CAPONE, T. & WEICHERT, V. (1973) A new antagonist treatment program for narcotic addicts. *Journal of Drug Education*, **3**, 4–7.

——, —— & —— (1974) Nassau county pioneers work release program for addicted inmates. *American Journal of Corrections*, **26**, 16–18.

——, —— & —— (1977a) Naltrexone and cyclazocine. *Archives of General Psychiatry*, **34**, 1181–1184.

——, —— & —— (1977b) Antagonist treatment clinic: long term management approach to opiate dependence. *NCMC Proceedings*, **4**, 4.

——, HENDERSON, R. K., CAPONE, T., et al (1984) Naltrexone treatment in a jail work release program. *Journal of Clinical Psychology*, **45**, 49–52.

——, CAPONE, T. & CAPONE, D. (1988) Naltrexone: lack of effect on hepatic enzymes. *Journal of Clinical Pharmacology*, **28**, 64–70.

CAPONE, T. & BRAHEN, L. S. (1980) Client perceptions of two antagonist programs. *Journal of Drug Education*, **10**, 63–67.

GINZBURG, H. M. & MACDONALD, M. G. (1987) The role of naltrexone in the management of drug abuse. *Medical Toxicology*, **2**, 83–92.

GROFF, H. & BALL, J. C. (1976) The methadone clinic; function and philosophy. *International Journal of Psychiatry*, **22**, 140–146.

HAMILTON, J. (1979) Evaluation of a detoxification service for habitual drunken offenders. *British Journal of Psychiatry*, **135**, 28–37.

JASINSKI, F. P., MANSKY, P. A. & MARTIN, W. R. (1973) Naltrexone: an antagonist for treatment of opiate dependence effects in man. *Archives of General Psychiatry*, **28**, 784–791.

JOHNS, A. & GOSSOP, M. (1990) Drug use, crime and the attitudes of magistrates. *Medicine, Science & the Law*, **30**, 263–270.

KLEBER, H. D. (1973) Clinical experiences with narcotic antagonists. In *Opiate Addiction: Origins & Treatment* (eds S. Fisher & A. Freedman). New York: Winston.

NATIONAL INSTITUTE ON DRUG ABUSE (1980) *Project Connection Best Strategy: Narcotic Antagonist Jail Work Release Program, Strategy 4*. Rockville MD: National Institute on Drug Abuse.

TILLY, J., CORNISH, J., METZGER, D. S., *et al* (1991) Naltrexone and the treatment of federal probationers. *NIDA Research Monograph*, **199**, 458.

TUNVING, K. (1988) Fatal outcome in drug addiction. *Acta Psychiatrica Scandinavica*, **77**, 551–566.

6 Naltrexone in the prevention of relapse and opiate detoxification

COLIN BREWER

In 1846, when a way of making surgery painless by using ether was discovered in America, the news spread quickly, and the first ether general anaesthetic in Britain was administered about two months after the first American one. By contrast, naltrexone has taken about 15 years to cross the Atlantic.

The principles underlying the use of naltrexone in opiate abuse are very similar to those involved in the treatment of alcohol abuse with disulfiram. Naltrexone does not produce an unpleasant physical reaction if heroin has been used, but it does produce an unpleasant psychological reaction. If people use heroin while taking naltrexone, instead of getting 'high', they find that nothing happens: it consequently seems rather a pointless exercise, and they are consequently deterred from repeating it. They do, of course, try to avoid taking naltrexone, just as people try to avoid taking disulfiram. Azrin (see p. 27) and Heather (see p. 12) provide evidence that careful supervision of the use of disulfiram improves the effectiveness of treatment with it, and that such supervision is vital. Exactly the same applies to naltrexone: if it is not supervised, it will generally not be taken. Accordingly, it is important to know some of the techniques of evasion that patients use in these circumstances.

Evasion techniques

There are no systematic reports describing the methods used by patients taking naltrexone to evade their medication, but the evasion techniques appear to be similar to those reported for supervised disulfiram (Brewer, 1986). Out of a cohort of 84 people, 45% took disulfiram regularly for at least six months under supervision and presented no problems.

However, 11% tried to persuade the supervisor that they could be trusted to take disulfiram unsupervised. Some of them may genuinely have believed this, but if so, their faith in themselves was misplaced. Three per cent were sufficiently inventive to try to exchange the tablets for something that looked like disulfiram. At one time, Antabuse, the standard brand of disulfiram, was marketed as a plain, white, scored tablet which looked like a form of aspirin, and some patients found that if they substituted aspirin, nobody noticed. Naltrexone is more difficult to substitute because it is a rather distinctive peach-coloured tablet; nevertheless, some patients have managed to find a tablet that looks something like naltrexone, and clinicians must be aware of this ruse. A further 3% of patients induced vomiting. Most people do not like to make themselves sick and it is an unpopular evasion technique, but it does occur. If it happens, patients should stay under the care of the supervisor for at least 15 minutes to permit absorbtion. Since both naltrexone and disulfiram have relatively prolonged effects, supervision can usually be done on a thrice- or twice-weekly schedule, as described by Brahen (see p. 47). Before long, a depot preparation may further simplify the task of supervision.

In Brewer's (1986) study, 24% tried drinking while on disulfiram. Strictly speaking, this behaviour is not so much evasion as testing-out, but in most cases, these patients evidently hoped that the warnings they had received were a bluff, or that the reaction would not be severe. Sometimes, they were right about the severity (see p. 42). A rather higher proportion of patients taking naltrexone can be expected to try using opiates, because, unlike with disulfiram, if they test it out, they do not make themselves ill; they just waste money. However, if they do try to use opiates, this may not be an unfavourable development, because patients often report a greatly improved sense of security when they discover that naltrexone really does block the effects of heroin.

Naltrexone in detection of relapse

Naltrexone is usually prescribed in the hope that if addicts do not use opiates for long enough, they may eventually change their habits of opiate-related thought and behaviour, but it can also be used for detecting relapse. Detection of relapse normally involves either urine or hair testing or searching for clinical signs of drug abuse, such as needle tracks, constricted pupils, etc. Urine testing, however, is expensive, undignified, inconvenient, and not too difficult to evade. Hair testing (see p. 99) lacks these disadvantages, but the results are not, at present, rapidly available.

A simpler and cheaper alternative method of detecting relapse is to use intermittent naltrexone. For example, in the case of a patient who has been 'clean' on naltrexone for about six months, an arrangement may be suggested in which he will agree to take naltrexone in a dose of 12.5 mg (a quarter of a tablet) at random, every one or two weeks, under supervision. If the patient has relapsed and become re-addicted, then swallowing even a small dose of naltrexone will precipitate withdrawal symptoms, usually in about five minutes. The patient is therefore faced with a disagreeable choice: either he swallows the naltrexone and will rapidly go into an acute withdrawal state, or he admits that he has relapsed. Relapse can thus be reliably detected within quite a short time of its occurrence, so that there is more chance to intervene. The consequences of swallowing naltrexone when re-addicted must be carefully explained, although in our programme, many patients understand these from personal experience, because most of them take naltrexone following naltrexone-precipitated rapid withdrawal. Few patients take the risk of swallowing naltrexone when they know they are addicted.

Improving compliance

It is very important to improve compliance with naltrexone treatment, so far as possible. The principles are the same as those enunciated by Azrin for disulfiram (see p. 21). First, there must be involvement of other people and taking the drug must be supervised directly. Appropriate supervisors include the family, counsellors, probation officers, next-door neighbours, clergymen – almost anyone with whom the patient has a useful relationship and whom he/she cannot easily avoid.

Secondly, it is important to have two-way communication, to make sure both that the supervisor is given necessary information and that this person realises that one of his/her tasks is to act as a kind of health visitor or community psychiatric nurse. He/she should be trained not only to administer naltrexone regularly, but also to report back at the first sign of any problem, because the sooner one can intervene, the sooner it may be possible to get any such problem under control.

Thirdly, as with disulfiram, it is important that naltrexone be dissolved before administration. It is to be hoped that the drug will one day be produced in liquid form, as it is rather difficult to dissolve, unlike Antabuse tablets, which break up in water in about 10 seconds. Naltrexone also has an extremely bitter taste, so it is particularly important to make sure that it is dissolved in an adequate quantity of liquid, preferably something that is fairly strongly flavoured. If that is not feasible – and some patients genuinely find it very unpleasant to swallow – then the next best technique is to break each tablet into three or four pieces, and inspect the mouth after swallowing. This is tedious (and some people would say somewhat degrading), but it is less degrading than relapsing into heroin use again.

Rapid withdrawal

At one time, naltrexone was only given to people who had been demonstrably opiate-free for several days – a week in the case of methadone or three days in the case of heroin. If they are still addicted and are given naltrexone, then withdrawal symptoms will be precipitated quite quickly, but several US authors have used this phenomenon to speed up the withdrawal process. Even in patients using quite large doses of opiates, whether methadone or heroin, these withdrawal symptoms can be controlled with a variety of drugs. The principle is to precipitate withdrawal symptoms, but to compress the worst of them into a day or two. If the patients are treated during that period with anti-withdrawal drugs such as clonidine, or with sedatives – usually benzodiazepines – then the most distressing aspects of the process will be over quite quickly, and if lucky, the patient may even sleep through part of it.

In one sense, there is nothing new about this procedure: heavy sedation has been used to help people through the withdrawal process since the 1930s (Kleber & Riordan, 1984), but without naltrexone, they may have to be kept heavily sedated for five or six days. This is very labour-intensive in terms of nursing, and not without its risks: the longer patients are sedated, the greater is the risk of pneumonia or other complications.

Several US studies have shown that the whole detoxification process can in fact be speeded up safely (Kleber & Kosten, 1984; Charney *et al*, 1986; Vining *et al*, 1988). There have also been cases of accidental ingestion of naltrexone by people on methadone maintenance, or people taking heroin who swallowed what they thought was methadone mixture but turned out to be naltrexone mixture. The results were unpleasant, but no more than that (Tornabene, 1974).

Brewer *et al* (1988) reported a study describing initial findings with a two- and three-day detoxification programme for opiate addicts using naltrexone, clonidine, and sedation. The more rapidly the dose of naltrexone was increased, the more the withdrawal process could be speeded up, and contrary to expectation, smaller total doses of sedatives and clonidine were then needed. More anti-withdrawal medication may be used during the first day, but because the withdrawal process is then completed more quickly, the total dose of clonidine and sedatives is rather less: the differences in the doses used were statistically highly significant. Speeding up withdrawal does not generally mean using very large doses of sedatives; compared with the total doses used in some chlordiazepoxide withdrawal programmes, where high doses of that drug are given for anything up to ten days (Drummond *et al*, 1989), the doses used in this programme are modest.

Following our study (detailed above), in which patients needed an average of two and a half days from admission to discharge, we felt that we could safely speed up the increase in naltrexone dosage, as described by Vining *et al* (1988). Instead of starting with 1 mg or 2 mg of naltrexone, a quarter of a naltrexone tablet (12.5 mg) is given, which is said to be enough to block all the opiate receptors. Naltrexone is a competitive opiate antagonist. Therefore, if any serious problems should occur and it was decided to reverse the withdrawal, it should only be necessary to give an adequate dose of opiates, and any withdrawal symptoms would be quickly aborted. With a larger dose of naltrexone, the dose of opiates would clearly have to be proportionately higher, to overcome the receptor blockade: in practice, reversal of the blockade has never been necessary.

Vining *et al* gave all their patients an intramuscular naloxone challenge, using 0.8 mg, and patients subsequently scoring less than 20 on the Wang Withdrawal Scale (Wang *et al*, 1974) were regarded as suitable for a starting dose of 12.5 mg naltrexone and for out-patient or day-patient treatment. Most of the patients in our study had too severe a reaction to the naloxone challenge to be regarded as suitable for this arrangement, but all but three out of over 150 treated with this ultra-rapid technique (Brewer & Mathew, 1989) were fit to return to the care of their families within 30 hours of starting detoxification. It was popular with patients for two reasons. Firstly, most patients had little or no recollection of their stay in hospital. This seems more likely to have been due to the acceleration of the withdrawal process than to the doses of benzodiazepines, which were not very different from those used in the slower method. Confusion is rarely encountered during ordinary opiate withdrawal. However, it has been reported after accidental ingestion of naltrexone by opiate addicts (Tornabene, 1974), and classic delirium has quite often been observed following a naloxone challenge.

Secondly, because the accommodation and nursing costs are usually by far the most expensive component of in-patient withdrawal programmes, being able to limit in-patient treatment to 30 hours in most cases meant that the costs could be reduced to a level which most ordinary families could afford. Indeed, this was the main reason for trying to improve on our original technique. In-patient costs do not matter so much if patients have health insurance, but most patients in Britain do not, and many health-insurance policies do not cover addiction. Therefore, anything that gets them out of hospital quickly and back, if possible, into the care of their family is to their advantage.

However, although popular with patients, the ultra-rapid technique requires rather intensive nursing; for instance, diarrhoea is common during withdrawal. With the slower technique, patients could generally get to the bathroom when they needed to empty their bowels or bladder, whereas with the ultra-rapid technique, the degree of confusion meant that changes of bed-linen were quite often needed. One patient suffered a cardiac arrest, some 20 hours after the start of detoxification and 8 hours after his last sedative dose. Because of earlier restlessness, he had received moderate doses of chlorpromazine and amylobarbitone as well, but had responded to questions an hour or two before the arrest. Successful cardiac massage was performed, but he died from brain damage and aspiration pneumonia. Although naloxone is very widely used in anaesthesia and in the diagnosis of opiate dependence, it is of interest that death has occasionally been reported following its use in opiate reversal in non-addicts (Andree, 1980).

Apart from this, there were few significant medical complications with the ultra-rapid technique: two patients who had become somewhat dehydrated from diarrhoea or vomiting received intravenous fluid replacement.

The social characteristics of our group were fairly typical. Many came from working-class families, and many were unemployed at the time of detoxification. Some had had previous treatment, and the majority had drug-related convictions of some kind. On average, they were using 0.71 g of street heroin a day; about half of them were injecting their opiates at the time of detoxification. The duration of their drug dependence ranged from six months to as much as 20 years, with an average of 4.5 years.

Since 1991, we have used a technique which is a compromise between the rapid and the ultra-rapid techniques. Doses of 0.5 mg naltrexone are given every 45 minutes until withdrawal is established. After adequate levels of sedation and withdrawal symptom control are achieved, in most cases similar additional naltrexone doses can be given without aggravating the withdrawal. Once a total of 5 mg has been reached, individual doses are increased progressively to 1 mg, 2 mg, 3 mg, 5 mg, 12.5 mg, and 25 mg. Patients are told to expect a stay of 48 hours, but 40% of the first 46 patients were able to go home within 24 hours. Amnesia seems to be less marked than with the ultra-rapid method, but the nursing is much easier. There have been no medical complications with this intermediate technique.

During withdrawal, some patients experience restlessness which does not respond adequately to benzodiazepine sedatives. Rather than further increasing the benzodiazepine dose, phenothiazines are used – generally chlorpromazine in a dose range of 50–100 mg six-hourly as needed. Recurrent vomiting is also a problem with some patients: if it is not prevented by chlorpromazine, it usually responds to metoclopramide or hyoscine. Hyoscine or other atropinics may also help to relieve intestinal colic and diarrhoea (Kleber & Kosten, 1984). Before discharge, patients are given 150–200 mg naltrexone, if they can tolerate it. That dose gives protection against relapse for three to four days immediately after withdrawal, which is one of the most vulnerable periods and a time when relapse is particularly likely to occur.

This has been shown, for example, in follow-up studies from the Maudsley Hospital. Within a week of discharge from the methadone-withdrawal programme, 50% of their patients were using opiates again, which is a disappointing result after three weeks of intensive in-patient treatment; many of them did so the very day they left the hospital (Gossop *et al*, 1987*a*,*b*). After a large dose of naltrexone, however, they cannot do that, or if they do so, they do not re-addict themselves. By three to four days after naltrexone detoxification, most patients are feeling reasonably well.

In a telephone follow-up of a sample of 22 rapid detoxification patients taken at random more than three months after discharge, only three said they had relapsed within the first week. Six patients stopped naltrexone at between four and ten weeks, and of those, three requested methadone maintenance, so that they remained in treatment. Eight patients stopped naltrexone during that period, but claimed to be remaining drug-free, while five were still taking naltrexone. These figures are not discouraging.

Post-withdrawal management

After the withdrawal stage, the principle of minimum intervention, as described by Azrin (see p. 27), should be followed. For alcoholic patients who have a reasonably stable relationship with someone, giving disulfiram and making sure that they take it is essentially all they need. It may be useful for them to see a professional worker from time to time, but they do not generally need intensive psychotherapy. The placebo or non-specific effects of such encounters are evidently considerable (Sloane *et al*, 1975; Brewer & Lait, 1980).

Much the same is true for naltrexone, except that probably a rather higher proportion of opiate addicts need the kind of individual therapy which is necessary for some alcohol abusers. However, many heroin addicts have little serious underlying psychopathology; they use heroin for the same reasons that people use alcohol – because for their group, it is normal, comparable to having a glass of wine at lunchtime. Unfortunately, there are numerous urban areas in the UK and other countries where for many people, using heroin is not seen as a particularly deviant behaviour. This should not be altogether surprising. A hundred years ago there was nothing deviant about using opiates in the UK, and the principal opium-eating part of the country was East Anglia, where opium was commonly added to the local beer (Berridge & Edwards, 1987).

Patients are usually seen two to four days after discharge, and again after about two weeks. They are then advised to attend, preferably with a family member, at four- to eight-weekly intervals thereafter for a year. The most important thing is to remind them and their families that if they encounter problems, they should seek help quickly and not wait for the problems to develop. It is more important to be available when patients need help than to see them regularly when they do not.

The need for additional psychological, social, or pharmacological treatments can best be assessed when the patient has recovered from withdrawal. Many common symptoms such as lethargy, depression, or anxiety improve spontaneously within a few weeks.

Some patients require more than one detoxification, and here too, the cheapness of the rapid methods is important. A further admission for detoxification is not necessarily a sign of failure and can even be a sign of success. If somebody keeps trying, he/she needs encouragement, and it must be hoped that the intervals between detoxifications will get progressively longer, just as with alcohol. It is not necessarily a catastrophe if an alcoholic has a relapse and needs to go back on to disulfiram or needs readmitting, any more than it is a catastrophe if a diabetic occasionally has to be admitted because the diabetes needs stabilising.

However useful naltrexone is, it is rarely in itself a sufficient treatment. Although quite a number of patients need no more than someone to supervise their naltrexone, they need it supervised in the context of some sort of professional – or at least caring – relationship. Families can often manage these things as well as professionals, but somebody has to care. Somebody has to take responsibility for supervision and for monitoring progress. Given the frequently secretive nature of addictions, the latter often requires laboratory tests. It may also help the patient to remain in treatment if he/she is partly motivated by regard for the feelings of a professional or a family member, as well as for personal reasons.

The actual alternatives to rapid detoxification and maintenance with naltrexone have to be remembered. The failure rates from in-patient methadone detoxification, which is probably the best alternative, are in fact quite high. Even in the Maudsley programme (Gossop *et al*, 1987*a*,*b*), quite apart from the 50% who relapsed within a few days of leaving, nearly one-quarter did not even stay in the hospital for completion of the programme, and as far as out-patients are concerned, more than three-quarters of them dropped out before the end of the programme.

Perhaps in the future, withdrawal from opiates will not be the responsibility of psychiatrists and psychiatric nurses. In Vienna, Loimer *et al* (1990) have developed a very promising and humane set of techniques for detoxification under a short general anaesthetic with either thiopentone or midazolam, using large doses of i.v. naloxone initially to clear exogenous opiates from the receptors. Blockade is then continued with oral naltrexone. However, although this approach is probably the most humane yet developed, it requires access to an intensive care unit with appropriate medical and nursing staff and equipment, and patients still require at least 24–48 hours in hospital afterwards.

References

ANDREE, R. A. (1980) Sudden death following naloxone administration. *Anesthesia & Analgesia*, **59**, 782–784.

BERRIDGE, V. & EDWARDS, G. (1987) *Opium and the People*. New Haven: Yale University Press.

BREWER, C. (1986) Patterns of compliance and evasion in treatment programmes which include supervised disulfiram. *Alcohol & Alcoholism*, **21**, 385–388.

—— & LAIT, J. (1980) Some facts of therapeutic life. In *Can Social Work Survive?*, pp. 126–140. London: Temple Smith.

——, REZAE, H. & BAILEY, C. (1988) Opioid withdrawal and naltrexone induction in 48–72 hours with minimal dropout using a modification of the naltrexone–clonidine technique. *British Journal of Psychiatry*, **153**, 340–343.

—— & MATHEW, K. (1989) Naloxone and opiate addiction. *Lancet*, ii, 683–684.

CHARNEY, D. S., HENINGER, G. R. & KLEBER, H. D. (1986) The combined use of clonidine and naltrexone as rapid, safe and effective treatment of abrupt withdrawal from methadone. *American Journal of Psychiatry*, **143**, 7.

DRUMMOND, C. & TURKINGTON, D. & RAHMAN, M. (1989) Chlordiazepoxide, methadone and opiate withdrawal: a preliminary double-blind trial. *Drug & Alcohol Dependence*, **23**, 63–72.

GOSSOP, M., JOHNS, A. & GREEN, L. (1987a) Opiate withdrawal: in-patient versus out-patient programmes and preferred versus random assignment to treatment. *British Medical Journal*, **293**, 103–104.

——, GREEN, L., PHILLIPS, G., *et al* (1987b) What happens to opiate addicts immediately after treatment: a prospective follow-up study. *British Medical Journal*, **294**, 1377–1380.

KLEBER, H. D. & KOSTEN, T. R. (1984) Naltrexone induction: psychologic and pharmacologic strategies. *Journal of Clinical Psychiatry*, **45**, 29–38.

KLEBER, H. E. & RIORDAN, C. E. (1984) The treatment of narcotic withdrawal: a historical review. *Journal of Clinical Psychiatry*, **43**, 30–34.

LOIMER, N., SCHMID, R., LENZ, K., *et al*, (1990) Acute blocking of naloxone-precipitated opiate withdrawal symptoms by methohexitone. *British Journal of Psychiatry*, **157**, 748–752.

SLOANE, R., STAPLES, F., CRISTOL, A., *et al*, (1975) *Psychotherapy versus Behaviour Therapy*. Cambridge Mass.: Harvard University Press.

TORNABENE, V. W. (1974) Narcotic withdrawal syndrome caused by naltrexone. *Annals of Internal Medicine*, **81**, 785–787.

VINING, E., KOSTEN, T. R. & KLEBER, H. D. (1988) Clinical utility of rapid clonidine-naltrexone detoxification for opioid abusers. *British Journal of Addiction*, **83**, 567–575.

WANG, R. I. H., WIESEN, R. L. & LAMID, S. (1974) Rating the presence of opiate dependence. *Clinical Pharmacology & Therapeutics*, **16**, 653–658.

7 Behavioural interventions for underlying problems in addiction

KEVIN GOURNAY

Generally speaking, people who recover from alcohol and drug problems will do so without specific psychological help and many current programmes using a great deal of additional psychological interventions are in fact unnecessary.

My personal interest in this field arose not because I was working directly with people who had alcohol or drug problems, but because of my principal clinical and research interest in anxiety disorders, especially agoraphobia. I have encountered addiction problems in two ways. Firstly, while carrying out research into agoraphobia, particularly seeing about 200 subjects before a major controlled trial over six years, I noticed a high incidence of alcohol problems. More than 30 patients in that sample who were referred primarily for agoraphobia also had significant alcohol abuse. Secondly, my department sees about 300 patients a year, including a growing number who have been successfully treated for alcohol abuse but who still have residual problems connected with anxiety, social skills deficits and, occasionally, obsessive–compulsive disorder.

The purpose of this chapter is to examine how behavioural methods can be helpful in dealing not with drug and alcohol abuse directly, but with the problems which are often associated with it. For example, in a group of patients coming into an alcohol-treatment facility, Mullaney & Trippett (1979) found that 13% of the men and 33% of the women had clear phobic symptoms. Other authors have suggested that many problem drinkers have social-skills deficits, and there is a range of studies indicating a very high prevalence of depressive symptoms, anxiety, and panic disorders in any population of problem drinkers.

Although there is much less evidence of this kind with opiate users, indications do exist that these depressive and anxiety states are also common in that population. Common sense would seem to dictate that all of these problems need therapeutic management in order to achieve long-term success in dealing with either drink or drug problems. However, one of the difficulties is that we do not know to what extent anxiety, depression, phobias, and other psychological complaints resolve after the successful withdrawal of alcohol and drugs. A major problem in evaluating treatments for disorders like general anxiety and depression is in fact their high rate of spontaneous remission.

Thus, with all the problems and the treatments to be reviewed below, one must consider the possibility that in addition, abstinence *per se* may in some cases be all that is necessary to account for recovery from conditions such as anxiety and phobic states.

Alcohol abuse and agoraphobia

There are two ways of looking at the alcohol–agoraphobia relationship. Firstly, one can examine the prevalence of agoraphobic symptoms in problem drinkers. Secondly and conversely, one can look at the prevalence of problem drinking in agoraphobics. Quitkin *et al* (1972) estimated that between 5% and 10% of agoraphobics abused drugs or alcohol, and Mullaney & Trippett (1979), examining consecutive admissions to an alcohol-treatment facility, found that 13% of the men and 33% of the women had clear agoraphobic symptoms. Additionally, 28% of the men and 22% of the women in this sample were borderline agoraphobics.

These authors found that the mean age of onset of the agoraphobia predated the alcohol abuse, which suggests that many people who subsequently go on to develop alcohol problems do so because they initially used alcohol as an anxiolytic. Unfortunately, there are no long-term follow-up data to determine what happens when these patients are withdrawn from alcohol, and whether continuing abstinence would lead to a reduction in the agoraphobic symptoms. Likewise, Smail *et al* (1984) found 18% of their sample of alcohol abusers had severe phobic states, and that alcohol was perceived and used as an anxiolytic. Bibb & Chambless (1986) looked at a sample of 254 agoraphobics and found that 21% of them (18% of the women and 36% of the men) had scores which were in the problem range on the Michigan Alcohol Screening Test (MAST). Chambless *et al* (1987) have further reviewed the relationship between alcohol and agoraphobia.

Treatments for agoraphobia

This review of the treatments for agoraphobia will not consider in any detail the role of psychotherapy or psychotropic drugs. Dynamic psychotherapy is notoriously difficult to evaluate, and controlled studies of agoraphobia and psychotherapy are rare. As to medication, there may possibly be a role for psychotropics in combination with behavioural methods: some evidence certainly exists that tricyclic antidepressants may be useful for certain patients. However, despite their widespread use, the evidence for the effectiveness of monoamine oxidase inhibitors or beta blockers, over and above behavioural methods, is slender.

With regard to benzodiazepines, in a controlled study (Gournay, 1989) involving 132 patients followed up for up to two years, comparing patients who were taking benzodiazepines with others who were not taking them, those taking benzodiazepines had a higher drop-out rate and a significantly poorer outcome on all measures.

Choice of treatment

Which behavioural method should be used? Relaxation, while popular, seems to be a relatively ineffective behavioural treatment for agoraphobia. Indeed, Marks (1987) has argued that relaxation therapy along with psychoanalytic psychotherapy provide excellent placebo control treatments.

Systematic desensitisation and flooding must be viewed as anachronisms. For ten years or more, there has been much evidence that exposure in real life is the treatment of choice and that it is both effective and powerful, with something like a 70% success rate. However, there is one important caveat – follow-up should include drop-outs, relapsers, refusers of treatment, and treatment failures. The literature indicates that even with a powerful treatment like exposure, the 70% success rate refers to patients who completed an adequate trial of treatment. If we take into consideration patients who drop out or are refused, or for whom the treatment is unpalatable, that success rate diminishes to something below 50%. This is a general point about outcome measures and selection of samples in the evaluation of treatment. Few papers report on the fate of drop-outs and refusers: these people are difficult to study, but they can be followed up.

As to the components of exposure treatment, there is no substitute for the patient practising in real life, in a graded fashion, exposure to what they would normally avoid. Indeed, there is evidence that exposure is an absolute prerequisite for fear reduction.

It is for this reason that drugs like disulfiram and naltrexone can be such a useful adjunct to behavioural treatments, especially for anxiety and phobic states. By preventing recourse to alcohol or opiates, which are often used as anxiolytics, they make it necessary for patients to deal with unpleasant feelings in a psychological way. I agree with the suggestion made by Heather (see p. 15) that they encourage exposure to stress and distress and the development of appropriate coping skills in a state of normal consciousness. Furthermore, if abstinence is consistently achieved at an early stage of intervention, it avoids the risk that even minor relapses may interfere with treatment, and impair the experience of control and confidence which is often a major goal of treatment. Patients may also gain a more rapid and complete recovery from alcohol-related neuropsychological and physical damage.

Patients with anxiety disorders are often referred while still drinking excessively and it is said by the referral agent that if we would deal with the anxiety problem, the so-called underlying cause – the drinking – would go away.

Experience has indicated that the alcohol and drug problems need to be managed first. If disulfiram is used, I would want to see the patient taking it and clearly demonstrating abstinence for three months before starting behavioural anxiety treatment. That is not only to give time for withdrawal symptoms to settle and to help the patient adjust, but also to see whether spontaneous remission might improve problems like anxiety and depression. The idea that these are underlying problems which, if treated, will get rid of the addiction, is incorrect.

Exposure

At one time, treatment programmes entailed therapists spending many hours helping patients to enter the phobic situation, and travelling with them on buses, trains, and tubes. There is now a great deal of evidence, however, that self-treatment can be as effective as therapist-aided treatment. Ghosh & Marks (1987) randomly allocated patients to three groups: one group received traditional therapist-aided exposure, the second group had an hour with the psychiatrist and was given a copy of a self-help manual, *Living with Fear*, and the third group had an hour with a psychiatrist and a computer program which in essence contained the parts of *Living with Fear*, including all the instructions. There was an equivalent outcome between the three groups. Many behaviour therapists now feel that exposure with the help of the therapist should be reserved for patients with particularly difficult problems. For routine cases, the aim should be to give patients the right kind of advice, and then follow them up. Thus, patients now receive about four or five hours' total treatment time, including follow-up, rather than the 30 or 40 hours which were *de rigueur* 15 years ago.

It is known that long sessions of exposure are important (Stern & Marks, 1973), that exposure should be given intensively, and that rapid exposure is better than slow. A study by Yuksel *et al* (1984) showed that exposing the patient rapidly seems to do no harm, but at the same time, some of the early work suggests that there is no need to evoke anxiety. A co-therapist is very useful, but not essential. There are somewhat conflicting data on this from Himaldi *et al* (1986) in New York and from Cobb *et al* (1980) in London.

Breathing exercises

Simple breathing retraining, which teaches patients to stop their patterns of hyperventilation, can be extremely effective. This too is a brief treatment.

Bonn *et al* (1984) randomly allocated patients to either breathing retraining or placebo control: breathing retraining led to very significant reductions in agoraphobic symptoms.

The place of treatment

When therapist-aided exposure is being used it does not seem to matter whether the patient is treated at home or in the out-patient clinic. I examined this issue in a controlled study (Gournay, 1989) because of a widespread view that community-based home treatment is better than hospital treatment. However, there were no data to suggest that this was true.

Several long-term follow-up studies have now been reported of agoraphobia five to nine years after treatment, including measures such as behavioural testing and independent assessment: these show that treatment gains are maintained.

One of the myths about agoraphobia is that there is always an underlying pathology. However, Arrindel (1980) and Fisher & Wilson (1985) have shown very clearly that agoraphobic people are no different from matched controls, apart from their agoraphobia. Complicated multimodal treatments with various kinds of anxiety management exercises, relaxation, counselling, etc., do not seem to achieve better results than simple exposure alone. Likewise, assertion communication training does not seem to improve outcome, and contrary to widespread belief, agoraphobics are no less assertive than the general population.

Cognitive therapy

There is no evidence for the effectiveness of cognitive therapy, which seems to be an integral part of many packages for agoraphobia. Several studies have compared exposure alone with exposure and cognitive restructuring combined (Emmelkamp *et al*, 1978; Williams & Rappaport, 1983; Mavissakalian *et al*, 1983). All of them show that over and above simple exposure, procedures like cognitive therapy do not seem to have an effect. In the drug abuse and alcoholism fields, 'cognitive' psychotherapeutic methods now seem to have been added to the armamentarium of therapists along with primal screaming, relaxation training, etc., but it is worth questioning the notion that if we give patients complicated packages, their outcome will necessarily be better.

Social skills training

There has been a great deal of enthusiasm for social skills training, as part of alcohol- and drug-treatment packages, as a treatment *per se*, and as a treatment for accompanying social anxiety or social skills deficits. Common sense would argue that increasing patients' social interactional competence via social skills training is essential to the efficacy of long-term outcome, but there are several major problems with this view. One is with definition: social skills training is also called 'personal effectiveness', 'assertiveness training', etc. Many of the studies do not explain what social skills training actually constitutes, and the quality of the studies is generally poor.

Another problem with many of the behavioural packages used in treatment programmes for drug abuse and alcoholism is that social skills training is but one part of a whole combination of procedures, so that it is very difficult to see which strategies are effective. A search for controlled studies of outcome, using specific social skills strategies in specific populations of people with drug and alcohol problems, adequate follow-up, and specificity in the components of social skills training, reveals nothing in the literature. However, the conclusion can be drawn that the key components are: role rehearsal, feedback, feedback using videotape, modelling, coaching, and *in vivo* practice. But, in the literature, the components of social skills training are not explicit, and practitioners using social skills training in clinical programmes apply very different packages of procedures. When the outcome of social skills is examined, the crucial factor seems to be the presence or absence of *in vivo* practice. It does not seem to matter how much we help the patient with role rehearsal and feedback: if we do nothing about the real-life behaviour, we change nothing.

Obsessional, panic and anxiety states

About 2% of the general population have obsessional rituals or ruminations of a degree which causes some upset and/or interference with their normal activities. An excellent literature exists on the value of response prevention for obsessive–compulsive rituals: several authors have shown that behavioural treatment is effective for about 70% of those completing treatment. However, the early promise for obsessional ruminations of procedures like thought stopping and flooding has not really come to fruition: when looked at objectively the results of these are disappointing. There are, however, some early data (Headland & McDonald, 1987) which show that continuous feedback of ruminations via a personal stereo player leads to a reduction of ruminations. In this treatment, patients are asked to record their ruminations and to play them back to themselves for prolonged periods. This is probably a way of maximising the effectiveness of flooding.

Panic disorder

Panic disorder is an area which is important in the drug and alcohol field. Panic is an extremely common problem: a study by Costello (1982) in

Canada, carried out on a large number of people, showed that about 12% of the population have a panic attack in any one year, and panic complaints are very frequent among those who come into alcohol-treatment facilities. However, this phenomenon has not been studied adequately, in terms of assessing people when they enter treatment and following them through in the long term. Hodgson *et al* (1979) suggest that alcohol is used as an anxiolytic by many such people. One could therefore argue that if patients have a primary panic disorder and then develop alcohol abuse, and if the panic disorder is not treated adequately, these patients will relapse. However, long-term studies of the prevalence of panic disorder and how it relates to alcohol are not to be found in the literature, though Chambless *et al* (1987) have discussed panic disorder and anxiety in the review mentioned above.

Treatments for panic disorder

Breathing retraining has been used to stop patterns of hyperventilation, and pharmacological treatments have also been used for a long time, going back to the work of Klein *et al* (1964) who thought imipramine very helpful for blocking panic. Probably more in the US than in the UK, panic disorder is seen by many as a biological entity. In the UK some extremely useful work has been carried out by Salkovskis & Clarke (1986), who arrived at a 'cognitive' model of panic, dealing with panic disorder in two ways. Firstly, they attack the hyperventilation by training the patients to hyperventilate and to recognise the symptoms which evolve from this, and then training patients to breathe correctly so that they breathe their way out of the hyperventilation. At the same time, these procedures are linked with a systematic programme of helping patients to change the catastrophic nature of their cognitions. Panic disorder is thus an area where much effort is being concentrated on evolving cognitive treatment strategies, and there are claims that this combination is effective for between 80% and 90%. However, we must wait for evidence from long-term controlled studies before this claim can be fully evaluated.

Non-specific anxiety

There are a number of common treatment regimes for general anxiety disorders, among which relaxation training has long been popular. Cognitive therapy, as developed by Beck, is now a very popular treatment, and anxiety-management training seems to form part of occupational-health programmes with stress-management procedures. It is an integral part of many alcohol- and drug-treatment facilities, together with psychotherapy: the combination results in there being major problems in measuring effectiveness. Difficulties connected with the prescribing of benzodiazepines in this area are well known.

When examined critically, behavioural treatments in this area do not show so good an outcome as some reports would have one believe. Where anxiety-management training and cognitive therapy are concerned, there is, so far, little in the way of long-term evidence from controlled trials that these techniques are as effective as they are with more clearly delineated states of neurotic depression. There are statistical differences in some of the studies that show a superiority of cognitive-therapy packages, or anxiety-management training, over placebo, but they are very marginal. There is no case at the moment for suggesting that they should be a vital part of any alcohol or drug treatment programme, particularly in view of the very high rate of spontaneous remission of general anxiety disorders.

On the other hand, some exciting work has been reported by Williams *et al* (1988) on an information-processing model of anxiety. This is reflected also by the work of Foa (e.g. Foa & Kozak, 1986) and Lang (e.g. Lang, 1985) in the US. Attempts are now being made to evolve genuinely cognitive treatments for these complaints but they are still at a theoretical stage, and it will probably be many years before a new, adequate cognitive package is available. There are other indications for behavioural psychotherapy but the main problems associated with drug and alcohol abuse are anxiety disorders, particularly panic attacks and agoraphobia, social phobias, and social skills problems.

Conclusions

There is good evidence that some people, particularly those with alcohol problems, have secondary psychological problems which can be helped by behavioural methods. It can be argued that in such populations, these adjuvant methods may improve long-term outcome. However, specific controlled trials with long-term follow-up are needed, and these have not yet been done. Overall, behavioural methods are helpful, but they should be used judiciously, and perhaps only after time and appropriate treatments have been given a chance to effect some possible improvement in the associated abuse of alcohol or other drugs.

References

ARRINDELL, W. A. (1980) Dimensional structure and psychopathology correlates of the fear survey schedule (FSS 111) in a phobic population: a factorial definition of agoraphobia. *Behaviour Research and Therapy*, **18**, 229–242.

BIBB, J. L. & CHAMBLESS, D. L. (1986) Alcohol use and abuse among diagnosed agoraphobics. *Behaviour Research & Therapy*, **24**, 49–58.

BONN, J. A., READHEAD, C. P. A. & TIMMONS, B. H. (1984) Enhanced adaptive behavioural response in agoraphobic patients. *Lancet*, *ii*, 665–669.

CHAMBLESS, D. L., CHERNEY, J., CAPUTO, G. C., et al (1987) Anxiety disorders and alcoholism. *Journal of Anxiety Disorders*, **1**, 29–40.

COBB, J. P., MCDONALD, I. M. & STERN, R. S. (1980) Marital versus exposure therapy. *Behavioural Analysis and Modification*, **4**, 3–16.

COSTELLO, C. G. (1982) Fears and phobias in women: a community study. *Journal of Abnormal Psychology*, **91**, 280–286.

EMMELKAMP, P. M. G., KUIPERS, A. C. M. & EGGERAAT, J. B. (1987) Cognitive modification versus prolonged exposure in vivo: a comparison with agoraphobics as subjects. *Behaviour Research and Therapy*, **16**, 33–41.

FISHER, L. M. & WILSON, G. T. (1985) A study of the psychology of agoraphobia. *Behaviour Research and Therapy*, **23**, 97–108.

FOA, E. G. & KOZAK, M. J. (1986) Emotional processing and fear: exposure to corrective information. *Psychological Bulletin*, **99**, 20–35.

GHOSH, A. & MARKS, I. M. (1987) Self treatment of agoraphobia by exposure. *Behaviour Therapy*, **18**, 3–16.

GOURNAY, K. J. M. (1989) *Agoraphobia: Current Perspectives on Theory and Treatment*. London: Routledge.

HEADLAND, K. & MCDONALD, B. (1987) Rapid audio tape treatment of obsessional ruminations, a case report. *Behavioural Psychotherapy*, **15**, 188–192.

HIMALDI, W., CERNY, J., BARLOW, D., et al (1986) The relationship of marital adjustment to agoraphobia treatment outcome. *Behaviour Research and Therapy*, **24**, 107–115.

HODGSON, R., RANKIN, H. & STOCKWELL, T. (1979) Alcohol dependence and the priming effect. *Behaviour Research and Therapy*, **4**, 379–388.

KLEIN, D. F. (1964) Delineation of two drug responsive anxiety syndromes. *Psychopharmacologia*, **5**, 397–408.

LANG, P. J. (1985) The cognitive psychophysiology of emotion, fear and anxiety. In *Emotion, Cognition & Behaviour* (eds A. H. Turner & J. Maser), pp. 49–63. Cambridge: Cambridge University Press.

MARKS, I. M. (1987) *Fears, Phobias and Rituals*. Oxford: Oxford Medical.

MAVISSAKALIAN, M., MICHELSON, L., GREENWALD, D., et al (1983) Cognitive behavioural treatment of agoraphobia, paradoxical intention versus self statement training. *Behaviour Research and Therapy*, **21**, 75–87.

MULLANEY, J. & TRIPPETT, C. J. (1979) Alcohol dependence and phobias: clinical description and relevance. *British Journal of Psychiatry*, **135**, 565–573.

QUITKIN, F. M., RIFKIN, A., KAPLAN, J., et al (1972) Phobic anxiety syndrome complicated by drug dependence and addiction: a treatable form of drug abuse. *Archives of General Psychiatry*, **27**, 159–162.

SALKOVSKIS, P. M. & CLARK, D. M. (1986) Cognitive and physiological approaches in the maintenance and treatment of panic attacks. In *Panic and Phobias* (eds I. Hand & H. V. Wittchen), pp. 90–103. Berlin: Springer-Verlag.

SMAIL, P., STOCKWELL, T., CANTERS, S., et al (1984) Alcohol dependence and phobic anxiety states 1: a prevalence study. *British Journal of Psychiatry*, **144**, 53–57.

STERN, R. S. & MARKS, I. M. (1973) Brief and prolonged flooding; a comparison of phobic patients. *Archives of General Psychiatry*, **28**, 270–276.

WILLIAMS, S. & RAPPAPORT, J. (1983) Cognitive treatment in the natural environment for agoraphobics. *Behaviour Therapy*, **14**, 299–313.

WILLIAMS, J. N. G., WATTS, F. N., MCCLEOD, C., et al (eds) (1988) *Cognitive Psychology and Emotional Disorders*. London: Wiley.

YUKSEL, S., MARKS, I. M., RAMM, E., et al (1984) Slow versus rapid exposure in vivo of phobics. *Behavioural Psychotherapy*, **12**, 249–256.

8 Methadone treatment of opioid addicts

LEONARD S. BRAHEN

Until the 1960s, opioid abuse in the US was controlled primarily by restrictive legislation (Peachey, 1986). Various treatment programmes may reduce illicit drug use, but on cessation of treatment, the majority of users return to illicit opiates in a matter of months (Hunt *et al*, 1971; Smart, 1983). Criteria for success, however, vary with different programmes and modalities. Some emphasise psychotherapy and abstinence, while others have more modest goals, such as reducing illicit drug use and other crimes or strengthening employment and family relationships. In such programmes, medication – primarily methadone – is often combined with psychotherapy and vocational rehabilitation.

Methadone: pharmacology and pharmacokinetics

Oral methadone is quickly absorbed, so that peak plasma levels occur within four hours. Methadone is largely protein-bound and is primarily metabolised in the liver to the glucuronide. However, there appears to be an accelerated metabolism for those in methadone maintenance programmes: various drugs may affect methadone metabolism, and renal clearance increases as the urine pH decreases. Phenytoin increases hepatic biotransformation and disulfiram inhibits it (Tong, 1980). Peak plasma levels of methadone are matched by maximum meiotic and analgesic effects. Methadone develops no tolerance to its capacity to diminish the agonist effects of heroin or to prevent withdrawal symptoms, but tolerance does develop to other effects such as analgesia (Goldstein, 1972).

Side-effects of methadone

Methadone appears to be free of serious side-effects at maintenance doses; any problems usually relate to pre-existing medical conditions. Minor side-effects such as sweating and constipation are not uncommon, but tolerance develops, and they usually disappear. Careful monitoring of dose and adverse effects can minimise any discomfort. Methadone does not cause or worsen abnormalities of liver enzymes; indeed, hepatic status often improves, probably reflecting improved nutrition and discontinuation of illicit drug use (Kleber *et al*, 1980). Levels of total serum protein, serum albumin, and total globulin may increase.

Entry criteria, dosage, and termination

In the past, before acceptance for methadone treatment, it had to be verified that the patient had an established history of opioid addiction and was currently addicted, and that previous attempts at treatment had failed. Counselling and psychotherapy were regarded as important components of treatment. Now, long-established, rigid entry criteria are being relaxed in pilot programmes in New York City to switch intravenous opioid abusers to oral methadone with minimal counselling (Yancovitz *et al*, 1991). Clearly, this is partly a response to increasing numbers of HIV-positive and AIDS patients among intravenous drug abusers. In our clinic at the Nassau County Medical Center, patients are fully informed about their methadone dosage, although in some other clinics, this information may not be given to the patient. When our patients want to increase or decrease the dose, it is first discussed with their therapist and then with the medical director. Clear reasons for the final decision are given to the patient.

In the past, firm criteria existed regarding the abuse of non-prescribed opioids, other illicit drugs, and alcohol, which served as a basis for discontinuing methadone treatment. The termination of patients from our programme has eased, along with the developing AIDS epidemic. Now, we frequently provide additional psychotropic drugs for such patients, who often have severe depression, anxiety, and insomnia, since methadone does not always relieve these complaints. Some patients have HIV-based organic syndromes.

Detoxification from methadone

The AIDS crisis makes it even more important that attempts at detoxification with methadone should be very carefully planned. We favour slow detoxification over several months, with special caution when the final, lowest doses are administered. With appropriate support systems, six months' detoxification has been more successful than the standard 21-day detoxification regime. Some programmes use naltrexone as a bridge to the opioid-free state, but simple, rapid methadone withdrawal alone has little value.

Efficacy of methadone treatment

There is general agreement that methadone maintenance programmes do indeed result in addicts taking fewer illicit drugs, although polydrug users may turn to other agents. Additionally, criminality is reduced and the work history is improved. Deaths from accidental and deliberate overdoses may also diminish. Long-term treatment is often required, however, for any semblance of success to be achieved (Newman & Whitehill, 1979; Gronbladh & Gunne, 1989; Zweben & Payte, 1990).

Additional drugs

Laevo-alpha-acetyl-methadol (LAAM)

LAAM, a long-acting analogue of methadone, remains under trial in the US and has also been studied in Holland. Its long half-life means it can be administered every two or three days, and it may also be useful for a subgroup of patients who metabolise methadone unusually quickly (Tennant *et al*, 1986).

Clonidine

Many symptoms of opiate withdrawal seem to be expressed through the adrenergic nervous system. Clonidine, an antihypertensive agent, is used to control the neural-outflow mediating part of the abstinence syndrome (Gold *et al*, 1979). It should be used for only a few days, however, since tolerance develops rapidly. Hypotension and sedation at effective doses may cause problems. Therefore, clonidine treatment requires admission to hospital or, for out-patients, intensive medical supervision. Not all withdrawal symptoms respond adequately to clonidine, notably insomnia.

Anxiolytics

For relieving anxiety and insomnia, benzodiazepines can be effective. Unfortunately, they have an addictive liability, which must be considered before they are prescribed.

Neuroleptics

Other than for psychotic patients, neuroleptics should be prescribed with caution, in view of their potential for provoking tardive dyskinesia.

Conclusions

Methadone maintenance provides benefits in the treatment of opioid addicts, while naltrexone can be helpful both for well motivated addicts and for non-violent addicted offenders who are on parole or probation. Disulfiram is a useful adjunct to methadone in the control of alcoholic opioid addicts (Liebson, 1973). Additional psychotropic medication, carefully prescribed and monitored, can be useful for deeply depressed, highly anxious, or psychotic addicts.

Acknowledgements

The author thanks Commissioner Harold E. Adams, CSW, Deputy Commissioner Raymond J. Condren, PhD, Myrtle Peterson, ACW, Director of Drug Treatment Services, Eugene Thompson, MD, Medical Director, Methadone Treatment Programme, and Ronald Melchionda, CSW, Director – Substance Alternative Clinic for their helpful comments and suggestions; and Eleanor Lisa and Carol Germano for their editorial assistance.

The opinions expressed in this article are those of the author and not necessarily those of the institutions noted.

References

GOLD, M. S., REDMOND, D. E. & KLEBER, H. D. (1979) Noradrenergic hyperactivity in opiate withdrawal supported by clonidine reversal of opiate withdrawal. *American Journal of Psychiatry*, **136**, 100–102.

GOLDSTEIN, A. (1972) Heroin addiction and the role of methadone in its treatment. *Archives of General Psychiatry*, **26**, 291–297.

GRONBLADH, L. & GUNNE, L. (1989) Methadone-assisted rehabilitation of Swedish heroin addicts. *Drug & Alcohol Dependence*, **24**, 31–37.

HUNT, W. A., BARNETT, J. W. & BRANCH, L. G. (1971) Relapse rates in addiction programs. *Journal of Clinical Psychology*, **7**, 455–456.

KLEBER, H. D., STABERTZ, F. & MERITZ, M. (eds) (1980) *Medical Evaluation of Long-Term Methadone Maintenance Clients.* Washington, DC: National Institute of Drug Abuse, DHHS publication no. (ADM) 81–1029.

LIEBSON, I. (1973) Alcoholism among methadone patients: a specific treatment method. *American Journal of Psychiatry*, **130**, 483–485.

NEWMAN, R. & WHITEHILL, W. B. (1979) Double-blind comparison of methadone and placebo maintenance treatments of narcotic addicts in Hong Kong. *Lancet*, **ii**, 485–488.

PEACHEY, J. E. (1986) The role of drugs in the treatment of opioid addicts. *Medical Journal of Australia*, **145**, 395–399.

SMART, R. G. (1983) *Forbidden Highs: the Nature, Treatment and Prevention of Illicit Drug Abuse.* Toronto: Addiction Research Foundation.

TENNANT, F., RAWSON, R., PAMPHREY, E., *et al* (1986) Clinical experiences with 959 opioid-dependent patients treated with laevo-alpha-acetyl-methadol (LAAM). *Journal of Substance Abuse Treatment*, **3**, 195–202.

TONG, T. G. (1980) Methadone–disulfiram interaction during methadone maintenance. *Journal of Clinical Pharmacology*, **20**, 506–513.

YANKOVITZ, S. R., DES JARLAIS, D. C., PESKOE PEYSER, N., *et al* (1991) A randomized trail of an interim methadone maintenance clinic. *American Journal of Public Health*, **81**, 1185–1191.
ZWEBEN, J. E. & PAYTE, J. T. (1990) Methadone maintenance in the treatment of opioid dependence – a current perspective. *Western Journal of Medicine*, **152**, 588–599.

9 The paradox of prohibition

JOHN MARKS

The Home Office refers to the ''Iceberg of drug dependency'' (Fig 9.1). Most of the drug takers in the UK do not come forward for treatment; most of them are not apprehended and prosecuted for their illicit acts; and most of the drugs coming in are not seized, in about the same proportion as part of an iceberg is above the water to that hidden below.

However, health administrators often choose to ignore this fact, and to concentrate on the former group, which is appropriate for doctors who are

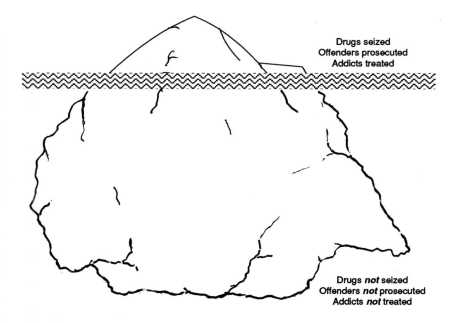

Drugs seized
Offenders prosecuted
Addicts treated

Drugs *not* seized
Offenders *not* prosecuted
Addicts *not* treated

Fig. 9.1.   *The iceberg*

treating people who want treatment. But if we are considering preventive health measures like HIV infection, and tackling problems that occur among those continuing drug use, then to ignore 90% of the problem seems rather foolish. However, the figure is probably nearer 99%, so far as problems presenting to the authorities are concerned. The group 'above the water' have come in for treatment, whereas the group 'below the water' burgle houses and cars, but, rightly or wrongly, they do not see themselves as having a medical problem. They treat their drug-taking as we treat our alcohol drinking, and they resent coming to see doctors, and even more so to see psychiatrists. It was partly because of this problem that prescribing clinics were resurrected in the Mersey Health Region, on the model of the Rolleston Committee's conclusions about prescribing by doctors to chronic, determined drug-takers (Departmental Committee, 1926).

On commencing my present service, I found a Rolleston-type clinic, basically giving out drugs to drug-takers. A host of questions immediately came to my mind. These questions crystallise down to variations on five themes:

(a) prescribing will undermine motivation
(b) it is better to treat someone than to give him drugs
(c) it will increase drug use in society
(d) how can we justify giving drugs to drug takers – why not drink to alcoholics?
(e) surely the drugs all leak out to others, anyway.

A stipulated condition of the funding of this service was that it had to be evaluated. Therefore Minnesota Multiphasic Personality Inventory (MMPI) pro formas were issued, and personal adjustment was assessed. However, the most significant part of the investigation was looking at the district of Widnes, just south of Liverpool, and comparing it with Bootle, just north of Liverpool. Bootle had the orthodox provision of an in-patient unit, out-patient clinics, counselling, and advice. Widnes had exactly the same. But the Bootle service did not give drugs out, as Widnes had been doing for a long time. I expected to find a greater incidence of drug taking, i.e. of new drug-takers per 100 000 population per annum, in Widnes than in Bootle. But in fact, the new notifications per 100 000 per annum in Widnes were 15.83, while in Bootle they were 207.6 – 12 times as great. It was the reverse of expectation.

At that time, in 1985, it was reported that the USA was spending $7000 million per annum on the most rigorous enforcement of prohibition in history. At the same time, it was also reported that in the USA, there were 5000 new drug-users every day.

In spite of the difficulties of notification, a general trend can be seen. Figure 9.2 shows the rise of notifications in the decades since World War II.

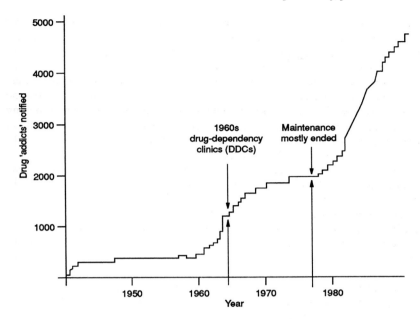

Fig. 9.2. Effect of drug-dependency clinics

Before 1960 there were no more than about 500 drug-takers registered in the UK, 0.001% of the population; there was then a steep rise, then a plateau, and then the notification rate rose dramatically. The orthodox interpretation of this is that it was due to some errant doctors in the 1960s, while the later rise, in the 1970s, took place following the Iranian revolution and the heroin brought in by refugees. However, that hypothesis begs the question it is designed to answer. What were these doctors or their equivalents doing in 1950, 1940, 1930, 1920? The question that needs be asked is – why did they start prescribing in this way *then*?

Probably, there was an innocent development: the advent of transatlantic travel brought a prohibition society, the United States, in contact with a relatively more liberal one in England. And so when the American refugees from their prohibition came over to Britain, restrictions were imposed. The same process has happened in other countries when decriminalisation or tolerance has drawn in drug-takers from outside. Therefore, the British prescribing system closed down, so that there was a relative black market, with a steep rise in notifications, and this was interpreted as the result of errant doctors' prescribing. As a consequence, the prescribing was restricted to consultant psychiatrists at licensed drug-dependency clinics, but an adequate ration was provided. This produced a reduction in the rise in notifications, until this rate became zero.

The theory that restricting prescribing is what brought about the fall in the rate of increase in notifications ended even prescribing at the clinics, which was done for moral reasons. Since the doctors in these clinics wanted to get people off their addiction, the number of notifications should then have come down, but that is not what happened. The *ad hoc* hypothesis of the Iranian revolution was used to explain that phenomenon. What seems more likely is that since there was a steep rise in notifications after the ending of general medical prescribing, doctors started to prescribe in an organised fashion at the clinics. This was mainly confined to London, and produced a fall in the rate of increase of notification. Then the prescribing ended again, and the rate of rise rapidly increased again. Thus applying an experiment, i.e. prescribing, produced an effect: a reduction in the rate of rise in notification. When the experiment ended, the effect on the rate of notification was reversed.

Stimson & Oppenheimer's (1982) long-term follow-up of a cohort of registered drug takers showed a 50–50 dichotomy between those still using drugs and those giving up after about ten years. It was Gaussianly distributed about that point. However, the important finding is that the addiction lasted for a matter of years, although a significant number of subjects had died. If this natural history is not understood, staff in drug-dependency clinics may have unrealistic expectations, and when these are disappointed, their morale may be badly affected.

The *y* axis of Fig. 9.3 is the percentage of the population in England who take a drug of social use (alcohol), and along the *x* axis is the age of that

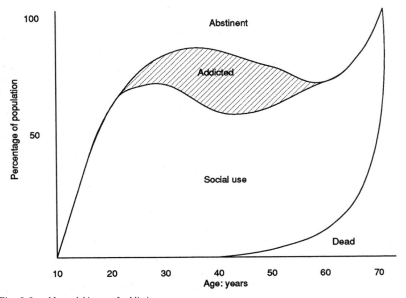

Fig. 9.3.   Natural history of addiction

population in years. There is a steep rise to a maximum in early adulthood, and then consumption of the drug for social use levels off. There are always a significant number who are abstinent. Because of an artefact of the way the graph is drawn, the horizontal axis rises up but the ratio of social use to abstinence remains constant.

What Vaillant (1970) showed for American heroin addicts and Edwards *et al* (1983) showed for British alcoholics was that this addictive 'set' persisted for ten years or more, as Stimson & Oppenheimer indicated, despite any extraneous intervention. Thus, whatever is done to addicts during that period will make relatively little difference – which is what any experienced hospital psychiatrist or prison governor would confirm: as soon as an alcoholic is let out of prison after 18 months, the first thing he does is to go to the pub to celebrate, or – in the case of the illicit drug user – to his dealer to 'score'.

At the drug-dependency clinic, we are confronted with youths who, despite alienation from their families, arrest by the police, imprisonment by the courts, the risk of lethal diseases like AIDS, beatings-up by gangsters, poverty, and loss of liberty, *will* continue to use drugs. So the actual choice that confronts the doctor when presented with one of these drug-takers (and they are the 90%) is not between them having a maintenance prescription for drugs, courtesy of the taxpayer, or coming in for treatment and getting off their drugs. The choice is: drugs from the clinic or drugs from the Mafia. They will get their drugs, one way or another. If we give them their drugs, then the 20-year-old, instead of dropping dead in a back street at the age of 21, survives until he is 31, when he may be able to become a full citizen again. We are not treating the addiction when we give drugs – we are continuing it. The justification for doing so is that it reduces the deaths, criminalisation, and other disastrous consequences of illicit use of drugs (*Lancet*, 1987).

In our sample, 22% who were traced after seven years, were off drugs, working, and had re-established their lives. Stimson & Oppenheimer found that this same proportion would be off drugs spontaneously, but only one of our sample died, and that was fairly soon after the start of the programme. In the long run, the number of deaths may well become insignificant – a very different story from the 16 deaths we might now have expected from Stimson & Oppenheimer's study. Therefore, the first rationale of the treatment, at least from the medical point of view, is that it shifts the death line to the right (Fig. 9.3). We do not see young people dropping dead in their 20s and 30s.

A local comparison of patients' criminal convictions in the 12 months before notification with the 12 months after notification showed a 15-fold reduction in acquisitive crime (Lofts, 1991).

Also, as there are more and more people using drugs, they become more normal, and this accounts for the large size of the iceberg 'under the water'. They have no symptoms or signs. They do not see their drug-taking as a problem, any more than we would see our coffee drinking or alcohol consumption as a problem. We cannot find any pathology. A very similar phenomenon occurred with tobacco usage; it was widely prohibited in England in the 1660s, but by two or three centuries later, a majority of the population smoked tobacco, despite the most rigorous prohibition. Similarly, there were less than 500 notified addicts in 1960; by 1970, they numbered 5000, and estimates of addicts' numbers are now conservatively put at 50 000.

What has been our response? In the early Victorian era, there was virtually no control of drugs. Arsenic, oxalic acid, and various other dangerous substances were available as 'cures', peddled quite irresponsibly by the druggists to a gullible public. Quite rightly, the government moved to protect the public from the promotion of such spurious nostra. This included opium, which was widely used by the population to soothe the awful rigours of the industrial revolution, with the result that babies were inadvertently overdosed by mothers wanting to go out to work. Hogarth's prints of Gin Lane graphically illustrate the consequences of gin being 'tuppence a pint' and laudanum available at every street corner. However, the Pharmacy Acts 1852 and 1868 required opium to be sold by a chemist, providing quality control, so that people knew what strength it was, because most overdoses were due to ignorance of the strength or adulteration of it by grocers. A label saying that the substance was poisonous, or – for those who could not read – a skull and crossbones, were sufficient to eliminate the problem. Thus, by the Edwardian era, long before there was any legalised prescription or other controls, opiate deaths represented an insignificant problem.

Then, for various reasons including American influence and military advice to control intoxicants, the situation changed: there were worries about munitions workers being drunk, and about soldiers taking drugs. The Treaty of Versailles said that all countries should control drugs, but left the nature of that control to each country. America opted for total prohibition of everything, including alcohol, and we know what sort of a society that produced. In fact, Chicago has now come to Liverpool: two policemen were admitted to hospital in the summer of 1988 after chasing a drug baron. But in England, around 1920, alcohol was effectively rationed in three ways: by a swingeing tax, by restriction of supply to licensed premises, and by restriction of their opening hours. At the same time, use of opium was restricted by medical prescription. The effect was dramatic: a drop in the cirrhosis rate by two-thirds and a great reduction in convictions for intoxication. This was probably the most successful example of public health legislation since Snow began the clearance of cholera from London in 1840.

Since World War II, in terms of the number of minutes an average person has to work to buy a pint of beer, the real price of alcohol has actually fallen. This ratio shows an even steeper fall for spirits. The restriction of access to premises has all but gone: one can get alcohol almost anywhere. Not only that, there is a sedulous advertising campaign telling us we must drink more.

The consequences of all this are shown in Fig. 9.4. The demand for drugs is shown on the y axis and the supply along the x axis. The horizontal

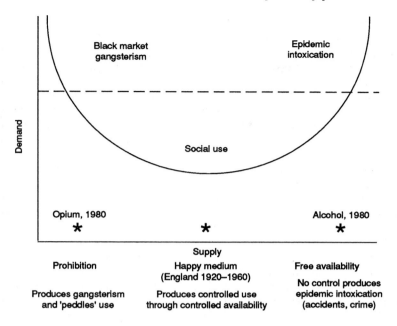

Fig. 9.4. Effect of controls on supply and demand of alcohol and opium

line represents the demand there has always been in all societies for an intoxicant: there is not a society in history anywhere in the world that has not used one, particularly for the externally driven proportion of the population – those who find it more difficult to cope with the random events of life without such help. If the supply is freely available, epidemic intoxication occurs as is now the case with alcohol. On the other hand, between 1920 and 1960, England had a happy medium, when both alcohol and drugs were effectively rationed. We have now gone back to relatively few controls on alcohol, and the consequences can be seen in almost any hospital ward: many road-traffic accidents involve alcohol, many beds are occupied by patients with alcohol-related diseases, and more than 50% of all cases that come before the law courts have an alcohol involvement (Royal College of Psychiatrists, 1986). Black-market gangsterism, with 5000 new users every day, is the situation in America, and now, since 1971, in England. It seems the opposite of what might be expected. One would expect the graph to be exponential – that demand (and so consumption) would be low when supply (and so availability) was low, but would rise as the supply rises as it does when we pass the minimum (see Fig. 9.4). As the supply is restricted, although there may be more determined drug-takers left, there should be fewer of them actually using. This graph (Fig. 9.4) should be exponential not 'U' shaped (quadratic). Why are there more addicts under prohibition?

If society restricts the supply of something for which there is a demand, then sooner or later, beyond a certain point, it will become worth a criminal's while to break through any sanctions and supply it at a higher cost. This is the rationale of smuggling. There is then a natural selection of smugglers, who become more ruthless and violent.

Exactly the same applies to a well intentioned piece of legislation, the Drug Trafficking Offences Act 1986, which purported to "confiscate the ill-gotten gains of drug traffickers". In practice, however, the least important members of the dealers' networks cannot prove that they did not get assets from drug-dealing profits, and so are guilty until they can prove their innocence. If they are removed, their share of the market goes to the major dealers, who have no problem in laundering huge sums of money through tax returns.

Nevertheless, even if the drug-takers left are more determined, they should be fewer. How is it, then, that a recent rise in numbers has taken place? It seems that if a drug-taker is spending £100 a day on a one gram habit at black market prices, he buys 5 grams. He then sells four grams, one to each of four users, to finance his own use, by cutting it, i.e. adulterating it to keep up the weight. He will get £80 of his £100 that way, and the remaining £20 will have to be obtained by other nefarious means such as burglary. But to get £20 cash, he must probably steal £100 worth of goods and get back a fifth of the value from a receiver. So the drug-taker must steal the whole value of his habit per day, in addition to distributing 4 g of adulterated heroin to others. We could not conceive, if we deliberately tried to do so, of a more socially destructive, individually criminalising, health-damaging, expensive, and *efficient* way of making heroin available than we do now, under prohibition. Having no legal supply, the state abdicates, by default, the source of supply to the gangsters.

That appears to be the explanation for the U-shaped graph: the supply-demand curve is quadratic, rather than exponential, as has always been supposed. The logical consequence of this is to be more restrictive if things are too slack, but paradoxically, to loosen up where things are too restricted. There have been some recent examples. The Dutch have decriminalised cannabis (*de facto*, not *de jure*) and Dutch cannabis consumption has fallen by 33% (Ministry of Welfare, 1985). Conversely, in the former Soviet Union, restrictions on the availability of vodka were too harsh and proved to be ineffective. There was an enormous increase in home brewing and distilling and a national shortage of sugar. Even before the collapse of communism, the government had reversed the policy (*Economist*, 1989).

It has been said that if someone went into a chemist and saw on the label of a bottle of cocaine that there was a one in a thousand chance of dropping dead immediately, and a 50 : 50 chance of being addicted for the rest of one's life, but a wonderful 'high', then only the people who take it now would take it anyway. In the Widnes clinic we prescribe amphetamines and cocaine as well as heroin and morphine, and we do not see all the youngsters in the community flocking to us. By and large, we see recalcitrants who cannot or will not give up their use of amphetamines or cocaine, and there has not been the consequent explosion that one would suppose.

Injecting cocaine, as opposed to smoking coca, or chewing coca leaves or having a brew of coca tea, is analogous to the contrast between injecting surgical spirit and having half a pint of lager. Alcohol is widely available in England, but there are not many in the general population who inject surgical spirit. Prohibition encourages, for economic reasons, the use of the most addictive and pernicious form of a drug which, given the choice most drug takers, even cocaine users, would not want – except for those who would do so anyway. Most of them would rather have the enjoyment they get from coca, but under their own control: they do not like being in pawn to the drug. If it were controllably available in the form of a 7% solution of cocaine, such as Freud or the fictional Sherlock Holmes used, then we would get controlled use. Active principles (e.g. diamorphine, cocaine, LSD) are probably best rationed through *pharmacists* to licensed individuals. The socially controllable equivalents (e.g. opium, coca and hashish) are best restricted to pharmacies but available for normal purchase. Even if it were argued that that is taking a great risk, it could hardly be worse than the situation already is in the USA.

Although we shall never get rid of private vices, such as drug- and drink-taking, we can reduce them to a minimum. The well intentioned effects of total prohibition appear not to produce that consequence, but rather the opposite. In criticising prohibition, what I am suggesting, and what Britain had at one time, until it was abandoned to our cost, is controlled availability. This is the happy medium, instead of having no control, in the case of alcohol, and abdicating control to the criminals, in the case of other drugs.

References

DEPARTMENTAL COMMITTEE (1926) *Report on Morphine and Heroin Addiction.* London: HMSO.

ECONOMIST (1989) Russia's anti-drink campaign. *Economist*, 23 December, pp. 52–56.

EDWARDS, G., DUCKITT, A., OPPENHEIMER, E., et al (1983) What happens to alcoholics? *Lancet*, ii, 269–271.

FAZEY, C. S. J. (1987) *The Evaluation of a Liverpool Drug Dependency Clinic.* Liverpool: University Department of Urban Studies.

LANCET (1987) Management of drug addicts: hostility, humanity, and pragmatism. *Lancet*, i, 1068–1069.

LOFTS, M. (1987) Policing the Merseyside Drug Treatment Program: 'The Cheshire experience''. In *Heroin Treatment – New Alternatives* (eds G. Bammer & G. Gerrard), pp. 97–108. Canberra: National Centre for Epidemiology and Population Health.

MINISTRY OF WELFARE, HEALTH AND CULTURAL AFFAIRS (1985) *Hemp Products.* Netherlands Fact Sheet, p. 2, 19E. The Hague.

ROYAL COLLEGE OF PSYCHIATRISTS SPECIAL COMMITTEE (1986) *Alcohol: Our Favourite Drug.* London: Tavistock.

STIMSON, G. V. & OPPENHEIMER, E. (1982) *Heroin Addiction.* London: Tavistock.

TREBACH, A. S. (1987) *The Great Drug War.* New York: Macmillan.

VAILLANT, G. H. (1970) The natural history of narcotic drug addiction. *Seminars in Psychiatry*, 2–4, 486–498.

10 Low-threshold and high-threshold methadone programmes

PETER GEERLINGS and JACQUES VAN LIMBEEK

In the Netherlands, the legal prescribing of methadone to opioid addicts was introduced in 1968; at that time, only a few hundred opioid addicts were using raw Chinese opium extract for intravenous (i.v.) injection. However, i.v. use of heroin became more popular in the early 1970s. Besides methadone treatment for opioid addicts, there is also some Dutch experience of the prescribing of lavo-alpha-acetyl-methadol (LAAM), clonidine and morphine to opioid addicts. However, methadone is still the drug most widely prescribed to opioid addicts in the Netherlands.

About one-third of the total methadone currently prescribed in the Netherlands is given to opioid addicts in Amsterdam. Of these 7000 addicts, one-third are of Dutch nationality, about one-third belong to various ethnic minority groups, mostly from Surinam and Morocco, and the rest are from other European countries. Approximately 25% of the Dutch addicts and 50% of the other European addicts in Amsterdam are i.v. drug users, whereas in the ethnic minority group, only a small percentage use drugs intravenously (Buning *et al*, 1988, 1990).

Methadone programmes

During the last decade, discussion about the treatment of drug addicts has been characterised by opposing views, which can be classified into pairs:

(a) medical versus non-medical treatment
(b) compulsory versus voluntary treatment
(c) opioid prescribing versus drug-free treatment
(d) low-threshold versus high-threshold methadone programmes.

However, the different programmes have tended not to define clearly what their positions were on those polarities. The low-threshold programme has as its main goal to keep contact with an addict by prescribing methadone without trying to change the addictive behaviour. The low-threshold programme has very few absolute requirements. Detoxification is not mandatory, continuation of drug-use is tolerated and no urine testing is performed. In this programme, medical care and information regarding HIV infection is given. The high-threshold programme is change orientated, involving counselling and urine-testing in order to change the addictive behaviour.

Development of substitution therapy programmes in Amsterdam

In 1968, the first methadone programme started as an out-patient service for opioid addicts; these patients came on a voluntary basis, and the treatment was free of charge. The goal of the treatment was abstinence, together with parallel improvement in the medical and psychosocial functioning of the addict. It was a change-orientated programme of a type which appeals to only a minority of i.v. drug users. When the heroin epidemic in Amsterdam became more widespread, a waiting list developed for this service.

This spread of heroin use became visible in the streets, in the form of increasing criminal activity and harassment of the public in certain central areas. As a result, the city council placed some pressure on the high-threshold treatment facilities to become more accessible to the addicts.

While these problems were increasing and the drug agencies seemed unable to develop a low-threshold maintenance programme, the city council felt the need to initiate their own service. The Municipal Health Service therefore inaugurated a system for helping drug addicts which had the goal of reducing the negative social effects of the drug problem. This low-threshold programme involving methadone by bus provided care for addicts who were not motivated to change their addictive behaviour, but who nevertheless felt the need to prevent abstinence symptoms due to irregular heroin use. Methadone distribution can be used not only for changing the addictive behaviour, but also as a major tool in care and in harm reduction or health protection, since each heroin addict needs a few other users as customers to support his own habit. Amsterdam therefore now has various methadone programmes with different 'thresholds'.

The lowest threshold project is the 'methadone by bus'. Once a day, two rebuilt city buses make a distinct route through Amsterdam, stopping at six different places in or near the 'drug-scene'. In these buses, liquid methadone is dispensed to heroin addicts who have been referred by one of the Municipal Health doctors. The conditions for participation in this project are:

(a) regular contact with a doctor (at least once every three months)
(b) participation in the central methadone registration system
(c) an agreement not to have take-home doses.

From the methadone buses, addicts can be referred to an out-patient, change-orientated methadone clinic, on the condition that they are willing to change their addictive behaviour, i.e. give up the use of illegal drugs.

In 1987, about 3500 addicts received methadone from one of the municipal methadone programmes in Amsterdam. However, in addition to the buses and clinic-based methadone programmes, general practitioners in Amsterdam also prescribed methadone to about 1500 patients. These general practitioners can be assisted by one of the doctors from the 'Consultation Project' of the Jellinekcentrum, the main treatment centre for addiction in Amsterdam. They are obliged to participate in the central methadone registration system.

Drug-free and methadone maintenance treatment and rehabilitation

The change-orientated treatment approach for drug addicts in Amsterdam is carried out at the Jellinekcentrum. These methadone programmes are comparable with other similar programmes in Europe or North America. The goal is to change the client's addictive behaviour and to improve psychosocial functioning. To this end, the client is regularly required to produce a urine sample, to investigate the possible presence of opiates and amphetamines. In addition, there is a requirement to attend counselling sessions. The Jellinekcentrum has out-patient detoxification and methadone maintenance programmes and an in-patient detoxification unit. The drug-free therapeutic communities in the Jellinekcentrum are comparable with the Phoenix House or Daytop model in the USA, which among other forms of therapy uses encounter groups to help change the addictive behaviour. The government has also funded special educational and work projects for addicts.

Outreach projects to contact addicts

To get in touch with addicts who do not seek help, three forms of activity are undertaken:

(a) street workers make frequent visits to places where drug addicts can be found, to give information about assistance
(b) doctors from the municipal health system visit local police stations twice a day to see arrested drug addicts; medical first aid, including methadone, is given
(c) a consultation team visits the general hospitals, where methadone is also prescribed frequently for detoxification or maintenance.

In 1987, about 2000 drug addicts were seen in the local police stations and 350 in the general hospitals. Others have contact with agencies such as outreach programmes to street drug abusers. In Amsterdam, approximately 70% of the total addict population of about 7000 persons has contact with the helping system every year.

In the low-threshold programmes, retention in treatment is given a high priority, with as few demands on the client as possible being made. The low-threshold methadone maintenance programme gained more interest in the light of the AIDS epidemic. In this programme more addicts can be reached for giving information regarding HIV infection.

Needle and syringe exchanges

In Amsterdam, the needle and syringe exchange began in the summer of 1984, during a hepatitis epidemic among i.v. drug users. In 1986, the Municipal Health Service started to make the exchange of syringes and needles also available on the methadone buses. In 1987, approximately 700 000 needles and syringes were exchanged at 11 different locations.

Only cautious conclusions should be drawn, however, from the first evaluation of the needle/syringe exchange programme (van der Hoek *et al*, 1988) since the data are based on self-reports, no testing of HIV was done and no follow-up has yet been carried out. Experience in the Netherlands suggests, however, that needle and syringe exchanges have been successful in attracting drug injectors who previously had not come into contact with any type of treatment programme.

Assessment of comorbidity

Until a few years ago, drug addicts in treatment were considered a relatively homogeneous group, all of whom required approximately the same abstinence-orientated treatment approach. However, in the last decade, it has become clear that a considerable amount of psychiatric comorbidity was present among addicts and was also an important prognostic factor in relation to results of addiction treatment (Rounsaville *et al*, 1986). In the Netherlands, opioid addicts have heterogeneous psychopathology. Using the Diagnostic Interview Schedule (DIS; Robins *et al*, 1981) to make DSM–III diagnoses, the proportion of opioid addicts with alcohol dependence, antisocial personality, or anxiety and mood disorders was very high. For instance, schizophrenia was five times more common than in the general population (Limbeek *et al*, 1992).

Implications for treatment

The implications of these findings are clear. In the first place, from a psychiatric viewpoint, the drug addict population is a heterogeneous group, which requires different treatment approaches. If addicts are to be treated more extensively, they have to actually come to a programme offering these services. Therefore, the first requirement is easy accessibility to the treatment programme for addicts.

The second requirement is a comprehensive treatment approach. This implies a functional combination of detoxification, psychiatric treatment, and social rehabilitation services at both the local and regional level. The goal of treatment should go beyond abstinence to include strategies for reducing the health risks associated with the continued use of drugs. Continuity of care is essential in order to have a significant positive impact on individual and public health. According to Bachrach (1981) the dimensions of continuity of care are: absence of time limits for treatment, easy accessibility to the treatment programme, a comprehensive approach, coordination of the treatment process (case management), ability of the treatment system to adapt to the changed needs of clients and circumstances (flexibility), creation of a working relationship with the client, and direction of the characteristics of these services primarily to addicts' individual needs.

References

BACHRACH, L. L. (1981) Continuity of care for chronic mental patients: a conceptual analysis. *American Journal of Psychiatry*, **138**, 1449–1456.

BUNING, E. C., VAN BRUSSEL, G. H. A. & VAN SANTEN, G. (1988) Amsterdam's drug policy and its implications for controlling needle sharing. In *Needle Sharing Among Intravenous Drug Abusers: National and International Perspectives*, pp. 59–75. NIDA Research Monograph 80. Rockville, MD: NIDA.

——, —— & —— (1990) The "methadone by bus" project in Amsterdam. *British Journal of Addiction*, **85**, 1247–1250.

VAN DEN HOEK, J. A. R., VAN HAASTRECHT, H. J. A., VAN ZADELHOFF, A. W., *et al* (1988) HIV infectie onder druggebruikers in Amsterdam: prevalentie en risicofactoren. *Nederlandse. Tidjdsschrift voor Geneeskunde*, **132**, 723–728.

LIMBEEK, J. V., WOUTERS, L., GEERLINGS, P. J., *et al* (1991) Aard, movang en psychopathologie onder drugverlaffden in behandelung. *Tijdsschrift voor Psychiatrie*, **33**, 156–174.

——, ——, KAPLAN, C. D., *et al* (1992) The prevalence of psychopathology in Dutch drug addicts. *Journal of Substance Abuse Treatment*, **9**, 43–52.

ROUNSAVILLE, B. J., KOSTEN, T. R., WEISSMAN, M. M., *et al* (1986) Prognostic significance of psychopathology in treated opiate addicts. *Archives of General Psychiatry*, **43**, 739–745.

ROBINS, L. N., HELZER, J. E., CROUGHAM, J., *et al* (1981) National Institute of Mental Health, diagnostic interview schedule. *Archives of General Psychiatry*, **38**, 381–389.

11 Methadone maintenance in the New York City jails

STEPHEN MAGURA, HERMAN JOSEPH and ANDREW ROSENBLUM

There are an estimated 250 000 heroin addicts in New York City, of whom only about 40 000 are in some form of drug-abuse treatment at any given time (32 000 in methadone maintenance and 8000 in others) (Office of Alcohol and Substance Abuse Services, 1992). Most of these addicts are committing crimes, and eventually become incarcerated for varying lengths of time at the city's central jail facilities on Rikers Island (Johnson *et al*, 1985; Sanchez & Johnson, 1987). Of all those arrested in New York City, 27% are using heroin, as shown by urine-surveillance studies (National Institute of Justice, 1988).

Since the early 1970s, narcotic addicts have been able to receive methadone detoxification at Rikers, in a programme initiated by Dr V. P. Dole. Out of a total of 80 000 admissions to Rikers, 16 000 addicts were identified and detoxified in 1986. Methadone maintenance has been available at Rikers since 1987. This is the only methadone maintenance programme in the US for incarcerated heroin addicts, and to our knowledge, one of only three locations in the world where methadone is available to prisoners. New South Wales, Australia, has a prison-based methadone programme, and doctors in the Netherlands are allowed to prescribe methadone for inmates. However, the Key Extended Entry Program (KEEP) serves by far the largest number of addicts.

About 80% of narcotic addicts at Rikers were not enrolled in a drug-abuse programme at the time of their arrest. KEEP is a route into methadone treatment for such untreated street addicts, and in addition, it provides an opportunity for continued methadone maintenance for those addicts who were already attending a methadone programme at the time of arrest. KEEP attempts either to interrupt the cycle of addiction or to prevent relapse, thus potentially reducing criminal recidivism due to narcotics use.

Facilitating the entry of incarcerated addicts into treatment, or retaining them in treatment, rather than merely detoxifying and releasing them after legal processing, is particularly important because of the AIDS epidemic (National Institute of Justice, 1989). At least 50% of intravenous drug users in New

York City are HIV seropositive (Des Jarlais *et al*, 1989). Anonymous HIV antibody testing of admissions to New York State prisons from the city shows an overall seropositivity rate of 20%, most of which is attributed by correctional authorities to intravenous drug use (Lambert, 1988). Since entry to methadone treatment is associated with substantial reductions in needle use, KEEP may also reduce HIV transmission (Ball *et al*, 1988).

The programme

To be eligible for KEEP, a new inmate must be diagnosed as a narcotic addict by a Rikers doctor and must be either a pre-trial detainee on a misdemeanour offence or a convicted misdemeanant serving a sentence of up to one year at Rikers. These restrictions on legal status are designed to screen out addicts who might be convicted of a felony and thus receive a sentence of more than one year, which would be served in a state prison where no methadone is available. KEEP has an obligation to avoid placing inmates on methadone maintenance who might be transferred to such a prison but unfortunately, this contingency renders the majority of addicts at Rikers ineligible for KEEP. In addition, once addicts complete detoxification, they may not be placed on KEEP.

About 3000 addicts annually receive methadone maintenance at Rikers through KEEP; 23% of these are women. KEEP is operated in three separately administered jail facilities at Rikers: the sentenced men's house, the pre-trial detained men's house, and the women's house (which houses all women). Women receiving methadone detoxification or maintenance are housed together, separately from the rest of the population. Male detainees receiving methadone detoxification or maintenance are also housed together, but sentenced male methadone patients reside on the general wards.

Eligible addicts who accept the offer of KEEP are maintained on 30 mg per day if they were not on methadone when incarcerated, and 40 mg per day if they were. (These are also the doses at which detoxification would begin.) Inmates stay at Rikers for an average of 45 days (ranging from one day to one year), until their cases are heard, bail arranged, or their sentences served. At release, KEEP patients have a referral arranged to a specific community methadone programme and are instructed to report within 24 hours. Community KEEP is operated under federal regulations as a 180-day detoxification programme. During this period, the patients are evaluated in depth and a decision is made whether to continue regular methadone maintenance, transfer to another type of drug treatment, or discharge from treatment.

How was KEEP established?

Prison and jail administrations at all levels in the US are generally opposed to providing methadone to incarcerated addicts. There are two main reasons for this. The first problem is the 'bad press' that methadone has generally received in the US, which is ironic, since methadone is a major means of drug-abuse treatment and has yielded favourable evaluation results (Simpson & Sells, 1982; Hubbard *et al*, 1983; Ball *et al*, 1989). The second problem is correctional authorities' legitimate concern about the practicality and possible danger of providing methadone in a prison setting (e.g. diversion of medication, violence, security breaches). Nevertheless, a convergence of the following special factors made it possible to establish KEEP in New York City at this particular time.

(a) A rapid increase in the New York City jail population, fuelled largely by increased numbers of drug-related arrests, leading to jail overcrowding and unrest. This has heightened awareness among city officials that new measures must be tried to treat addicts, in the hope of reducing recidivism.

(b) The AIDS epidemic, which also has created incentives for city officials to reach out to untreated i.v. drug users with improved services.

(c) The success of the ongoing methadone detoxification programme at Rikers.

(d) The personal commitment of drug-abuse treatment administrators, notably J. M. Martinez, Jr, former Director of the New York State Division of Substance Abuse Services (DSAS), who approved the programme; C. LaPorte, former Deputy Director of Chemotherapy Services at DSAS, who designed the programme; and M. Wishart, former Director of Montefiore Hospital's Health Services at Rikers, who implemented KEEP.

(e) The willingness of key correctional administrators to take a risk; these were notably R. Koehler, former Commissioner of the New York City Department of Correction, and Warden Levy of the women's house on Rikers, where KEEP was originally piloted with 50 women addicts.

The establishment of KEEP required the cooperation of diverse agencies to achieve a common goal, despite differences in their organisation philosophies and objectives. Fortunately, a major medical institution, Montefiore Hospital, was already offering medical and detoxification services to inmates when the programme was developed. However, new procedures to accommodate extended maintenance on methadone had to be created, new personnel hired, and facilities made available. The Department of Correction had to modify existing regulations about the management and living quarters of inmates involved in the programme, construct new medication stations and provide the necessary security. Community methadone programmes were enlisted to provide patient evaluations in continued treatment. The state's Division of Substance Abuse Services funded the programme and that agency's Chemotherapy Services Bureau developed the basic concepts and coordinated its implementation.

Preliminary evaluation results

KEEP has demonstrated that the anxieties which correctional personnel have about providing methadone to prisoners are largely groundless. Diversion of medication has not been a problem; the few patients who have attempted 'spit-backs' have been detected and dropped from the programme. There have been no conflicts between inmates who have access to methadone and those who do not. In fact, correctional staff perceive that inmates receiving methadone are less irritable and easier to manage than others. KEEP is now viewed as an integral part of the administration of the jail, and is accepted by the wardens as an essential programme for the treatment of heroin addiction and as an AIDS prevention measure among the jail population.

Of addicts who are offered KEEP, 95% accept and remain in the programme while at Rikers. This does not mean, of course, that they all have positive attitudes towards methadone treatment, nor that they intend to remain on methadone after release. Our research with these addicts indicates that some initially view KEEP simply as a way to make their incarceration more tolerable; they receive a substitute opiate and have medical out-patient status. Participation may not signify real interest in continuing treatment nor even create such an interest.

One indicator of whether KEEP is accomplishing its goal of recruiting addicts for treatment is the inmates' rate of reporting to community methadone programmes after their release. The numbers of KEEP participants served between 1 January and 30 September 1988 in three main categories are shown in Table 11.1. The reporting rate is defined as appearing at a community programme at least once (within 24 hours) after release. This rate is fairly high (73.5%), as might be expected if only because of these subjects' immediate need for an opiate to prevent the onset of withdrawal symptoms. An addict released from jail, often abruptly and with no money other than a bus fare, may well have difficulty in obtaining heroin at short notice.

TABLE 11.1
KEEP admissions, discharges, and reporting to community methadone programmes

	Men: sentenced	Men: pre-trial	Women	Total
Admissions	1361	455	548	2364
Discharges	1150	219	509	1878
Reported	876	160	344	1380
% reported	76.2	73.1	67.6	73.5

Source: Bureau of Chemotherapy Services, New York State Division of Substance Abuse Services.

TABLE 11.2
Reporting and retention rates – research sample (released subjects only)

	No show	Reported	Exited	Remaining
Men (*n* = 12)	3	9 (75%)	2	7 (58%)
Women (*n* = 22)	8	14 (64%)	7	7 (32%)
Total (*n* = 34)	11	23 (68%)	9	14 (41%)

Note: Status of subjects was determined on 15 May 1989, an average of two months after their release.

A better measure of engagement in treatment is the retention rate. Our research involves collecting prospective longitudinal data on a random sample of KEEP participants who were *not* in methadone treatment at the time of incarceration. (These are the addicts with the poorest prognosis after release.) We conducted 100 baseline interviews with such subjects at Rikers between 1 February and 30 April 1989, of whom 34 were released by the time we determined their status on 15 May 1989 (see Table 11.2). The overall reporting rate (68%) for these 34 released subjects is similar to that found for the 1988 KEEP population (Table 11.1). The retention rate, an average of two months after release from jail, is 41% and is lower for women (32%) than for men (58%), although the difference is not statistically significant due to small sample size. Follow-up of the entire research sample is continuing.

Discussion

The reporting and short-term retention rates of KEEP participants are similar to the outcomes for parolees referred to drug-abuse treatment by New York State's ACCESS project (Joseph, 1987). Forty-eight per cent of parolees reported to their designated programme, and entered treatment, but unlike KEEP participants, many of these were under some degree of legal compulsion to seek treatment.

Although the preliminary statistics for KEEP are encouraging, there are several serious obstacles to the retention of KEEP subjects in methadone maintenance. Most subjects can think of reasons why they might not wish or be able to report to a community programme; why they might not be enrolled should they appear; or why they might not remain long. The concept of guaranteed slots for them is good, but currently only 12 community programmes are funded to participate. Addicts considering entering treatment are likely to be referred to community programmes far from their homes and usually with limited medication hours. Addicts also are aware that enrolment in a community programme is not automatic. Applicants must produce suitable identification, which many simply do not have, and they must establish their eligibility for public assistance, in order that the programme may receive reimbursement; this requires both acceptable identification and following through with several steps of an application process. As one KEEP patient put it, "it's easier to cop drugs". The KEEP programme is aware of such obstacles, and has been attempting to begin the application for public assistance while inmates are still at Rikers. Hindrances to this have been the discharge of inmates before the process can be completed and lack of staff to pursue the labour-intensive tasks involved.

Most of the KEEP participants have considerable anxieties about remaining on long-term methadone maintenance. The most prevalent fears are that methadone 'eats the bones' (common variant: 'rots the teeth') and that it is 'hard to kick' ('too addictive'). This prevailing 'folklore' about methadone maintenance in the addict subculture has been documented previously by researchers in our organisation (Goldsmith *et al*, 1984). However, there seems to be no basis in the medical literature for fears about these specific long-term side-effects (Kreek, 1983). It has been suggested that these beliefs have some empirical basis in addicts' previous experiences while undergoing methadone detoxification and/or being maintained in the past on inadequate levels of methadone, both of which may cause withdrawal symptoms (Goldsmith *et al*, 1984).

Another major barrier to retaining these addicts in community treatment is their level of deprivation. Methadone-programme administrators have observed that, as a group, KEEP patients have more severe personal and social deficits than other addicts applying for treatment. At incarceration, most had no jobs or usable job skills and were literally 'street addicts', without stable living quarters or social support. Many of the women were earning their living, as well as drug money, by prostitution. The inherent instability of this lifestyle, as well as the influence of paramours or pimps, may help account for the women's lower reporting rates to community programmes. It is true that drug-abuse treatment can help an addict achieve stability, but it is also true that some minimal level of security is required to enable an addict to comply with the requirements of an out-patient drug-abuse treatment programme. Again, while drug abuse was instrumental in creating the difficult situations these addicts find themselves in, it is also true that merely enrolling in treatment will not automatically result in procuring adequate housing, adequate and legal income, supportive family and friends, etc. Methadone programmes generally have only limited abilities to assist clients in obtaining the social, vocational, housing, medical, and social therapeutic services they may need. As mentioned above, even securing acceptable identification is not a quick or easy task. Consequently, for these various reasons, one might anticipate early drop-outs of many KEEP clients from community treatment.

Lastly, there is the challenge to methadone treatment of the typical polydrug abuse patterns of drug addicts in the inner cities. (Polydrug abuse

TABLE 11.3
Drug use for heroin addicts not in treatment at incarceration (n = 100)

	Daily	*Weekly*	*Less than 3 times per month*	*None*
	Percentage using six months before jail			
Intravenous heroin	68	8	5	19
Intravenous cocaine	39	8	6	47
Speedball[1]	56	10	4	30
Crack (cocaine)	35	7	11	47

1. Intravenous heroin and cocaine.

seems common among addicts in the UK as well (Hammersley & Morrison, 1987).) Many of the KEEP participants are using cocaine in some form as heavily as they are using heroin (see Table 11.3), and about 25% say during their research interviews that cocaine (including crack) is their *primary* drug problem. Methadone programmes generally have no specialised therapies to deal with cocaine abuse, nor are there proven effective out-patient treatments for cocaine at this time.

One way we are attempting to improve the prospects for engaging KEEP patients in community treatment is to test the efficacy of short-term, one-to-one crisis intervention casework after the inmates' release from jail. This Intensive Transition Service (ITS) is intended to deal with the types of transition problems, described above, that KEEP participants confront at release, which could interfere with their reporting to or remaining enrolled in a community methadone programme. The effectiveness of both KEEP and ITS will be evaluated using a controlled pre/post-test experimental design, with funding from the National Institute on Drug Abuse. A sample of KEEP participants at Rikers will be randomly assigned (on a voluntary basis) to two study groups: regular KEEP programme ($n = 120$) or KEEP plus ITS ($n = 120$). A third study group, the controls, will be heroin detoxification patients with characteristics similar to those of KEEP patients, but who could not be enrolled in KEEP due to lack of space or technical ineligibility ($n = 150$). Outcomes for the three groups will be compared at six months after their release from Rikers, and these results should throw a more conclusive light on the outcome of patients dealt with by the programme.

Acknowledgements

The study was funded by Grant No. 1 RO1 DA05606 from the National Institute on Drug Abuse, in cooperation with the New York State Division of Substance Abuse Services. The authors are indebted to Charles LaPorte, Margaret Wishart, John Perez, Richard Marks, Lawrence Watts, Raymond Diaz and Thomas Longo for their cooperation in the conduct of this study. We are grateful to Dr Colin Brewer for the opportunity to publish this work.

References

BALL, J. C., LANGE, R. W. & MYERS, P. C. (1988) Reducing the risk of AIDS through methadone maintenance treatment. *Journal of Health & Social Behaviour*, **29**, 214–226.

DES JARLAIS, D. C., FRIEDMAN, S. R. & NOVICK, D. M. (1989) HIV-1 infection among intravenous drug users in Manhattan, New York City, from 1977 through 1987. *Journal of the American Medical Association*, **261**, 1008–1012.

GOLDSMITH, D. S., HUNT, D. E., LIPTON, D. S., *et al* (1984) Methadone folklore: beliefs about side-effects and their impact on treatment. *Human Organisation*, **43**, 330–340.

HAMMERSLEY, R. & MORRISON, V. (1987) Effects of polydrug use on the criminal activities of heroin-users. *British Journal of Addiction*, **82**, 899–906.

HUBBARD, R. L., ALLISON, M., BRAY, R. M., *et al* (1983) An overview of client characteristics, treatment services, and during treatment outcomes, for outpatient methadone clinics in the Treatment Outcome Prospective Study (TOPS). In *Research on the Treatment of Narcotic Addiction: State of the Art* (ed. J. R. Cooper), pp. 714–751. Rockville, MD: National Institute on Drug Abuse.

JOHNSON, B. D., GOLDSTEIN, P. J. & PREBLE, E. (1985) *Taking Care of Business: the Economics of Crime by Heroin Abusers*. Lexington, MA: Lexington Books.

JOSEPH, H. (1987) *An Evaluation of the ACCESS Project*. New York: Bureau of Research and Evaluation, Division of Substance Abuse Services.

KREEK, M. J. (1983) Health consequences associated with the use of methadone. In *Research on the Treatment of Narcotic Addiction: State of the Art* (ed. J. R. Cooper), pp. 456–482. Rockville, MD: National Institute on Drug Abuse.

LAMBERT, B. (1988) AIDS survey shows course of infection. *NY Times*, July 15.

NATIONAL INSTITUTE OF JUSTICE (1988) *Drug Use Forecasting (DUF): April–June 1988 Data*. Washington, DC: NIJ.

—— (1989) *DUF: Drug Use Forecasting to July to September 1989*. Washington, DC: NIJ.

OFFICE OF ALCOHOL AND SUBSTANCE ABUSE SERVICES (1992) *1993 Comprehensive Plan and Update*. Albany, NY: OASAS.

SANCHEZ, J. E. & JOHNSON, B. D. (1987) Women and the drug–crime connection – crime rates among women at Rikers Island. *Journal of Psychoactive Drugs*, **19**, 205–215.

SIMPSON, D. D. & SELLS, S. B. (1982) *Evaluation of Drug Abuse Treatment Effectiveness: Summary of DARP Follow-up Research*. Rockville, MD: National Institute on Drug Abuse.

12 Hair analysis for non-volatile drugs of abuse: a new technique for detecting and deterring relapse

COLIN BREWER

Regular urine testing is a feature of most treatment programmes. Given the limitations of self-reports of drug use, the lack of obvious intoxication which is a feature of certain types of abuse, and the well documented tendency of addicts to deceive themselves as well as others, such testing is often important both for monitoring the progress of individual patients and for assessing the effectiveness of particular interventions.

In the USA, the federal regulations governing methadone programmes require testing every two weeks on average; the additional requirement in most programmes for patients to attend daily to consume their methadone makes frequent urine sampling relatively easy. Not surprisingly, it has been shown that random rather than regular and predictable sampling gives higher detection rates (Harford & Kleber, 1978; Brewer, 1988). Even so, attempts at evasion by determined, desperate, or merely mischievous patients are a persistent and troublesome problem, and the consequent need for personnel to observe the actual passage of urine from bladder to container can be embarrassing and humiliating for both parties, as well as time consuming. Some patients find it genuinely difficult to pass urine under observation, even when they have no illicit drug use to conceal.

In Britain, where patients usually collect their methadone from an ordinary commercial neighbourhood pharmacy and only visit a clinic once every week or two, the possibilities of concealing the use of unprescribed drugs are much greater. The same is true of non-pharmacological out-patient programmes. Where a positive result could have particularly serious consequences – being charged with a breach of probation or losing a job, for example – patients have been known to use very ingenious methods of evasion, including filling their bladder with 'clean' urine by self-catheterisation.

Furthermore, a positive urine specimen says little about the pattern of unprescribed drug use. For example, finding morphine in the urine of methadone patients might indicate simply that they occasionally used small amounts and happened to have done so the previous night; or that they were regularly using large amounts but had thought it wise not to use heroin for two or three days before their scheduled visit. Urine tests are rarely quantitative but even quantitative urine tests are of little value in this situation.

Fortunately, most non-volatile drugs are incorporated into the matrix of body hair in concentrations which, though small, are detectable and measurable with sensitive modern techniques (Baumgartner *et al*, 1989; Nakahara *et al*, 1991; Fritch *et al*, 1992). Hair has been likened to a chemical tape recorder. It has been known for many years that certain toxic elements, such as arsenic, could be detected in hair, but only in the last 10–15 years have techniques been devised for identifying and quantifying organic or pharmacological compounds. Since hair grows at a fairly predictable rate, the concentration of a given drug in a given length of hair provides some indication of the amount ingested during the growth of the portion being analysed. Animal experiments have shown a good correlation between dose and concentration for a number of compounds (Nakahara *et al*, 1991) and data on humans – although naturally more difficult to obtain in the case of illicit drugs of variable purity and strength – give similar indications (Magura *et al*, 1992).

As important as the ability to quantify drug use and to measure changes in intake from one month to the next, is the virtual impossibility of evasion. Few people are willing to shave off all their hair, and such behaviour in this context would attract instant suspicion. In any case, hair from any part of the body can, in principle, be used for testing. Obviously, the collection of hair samples involves minimal time and indignity, and entails no risk of infection with HIV or hepatitis. If a positive result is disputed, it is usually possible to collect a further sample from the same growing period and repeat the test.

Clinical trials

Several studies have shown that hair analysis is much more sensitive for detecting illicit drug use than urine screening or self-reports (Magura *et al*, 1992; Callahan *et al*, 1992; Mieczkowski *et al*, 1993). It is particularly useful for detecting irregular or occasional use, but since many relapses initially involve 'dabbling', it follows that hair analysis is a very sensitive method of relapse detection.

Deterrent and symbolic aspects

It is often said, in debates about preventing crime, that the certainty of detection is the best deterrent. Random and frequent breath tests for alcohol have often had significant deterrent effects on the incidence of drunken driving, while nobody who drives in the US can fail to notice that the majority of US drivers keep close to the speed limit because the ubiquity of radar devices makes for a very high risk of detection of speeding. The virtual impossibility of being able to use non-prescribed drugs without the risk of detection should therefore lead to a therapeutically useful change in the balance of power between patient and clinic staff, especially in methadone programmes and in probation-linked treatments. It may also be possible to find out whether patients who are allowed 'take home' doses of methadone, as is common in Britain and is permitted in some US methadone programmes, are actually consuming the medication themselves, rather than selling it or exchanging it for other drugs.

Economy

A single hair test can give useful information about drug use during the previous three months – or more or less – depending on the length examined. Although the technique is not yet widely used, it is not particularly expensive when done on a large scale. Typical commercial rates for US laboratories offering the service are $45 for a five-drug screen but existing services are generally targeted at employment screening rather than the monitoring of drug abusers in treatment.

Detecting drug abuse in sport

Drug abuse in athletes is a growing problem. Because of the considerable financial rewards, professional athletes often employ the services of biochemists to evade detection. A common practice is to use certain banned drugs only during training, hoping that no traces will be left by the time of the actual competition. Hair testing could make such evasion much more difficult.

Potential impact on the management of substance abuse

Current methods of assessing compliance with drug-abuse treatment are crude and inaccurate; this is in sharp contrast to the measurement of treatment response in many other conditions. In diagnoses as disparate as anaemia, cancer, rheumatoid arthritis, and hypertension, fairly precise measurements of improvement or deterioration are possible, and this has greatly facilitated the development of better treatments.

The difficulty of quantifying drug use has reinforced the existing tendency in some treatment programmes and philosophies to regard any drug use as a treatment failure because total abstinence is the only acceptable goal. However, in most conditions, patients and their doctors are generally pleased if there is a significant improvement in the problem being treated, even if the relief is less than total. If one of the goals in the treatment of heroin abuse is to help patients to abstain from heroin, using only a little heroin over, say, three months is surely preferable to using a great deal of it.

References

BAUMGARTNER, W. A., HILL, V. A. & BLAHD, M. D. (1989) Hair analysis for drugs of abuse. *Journal of Forensic Sciences*, **34**, 1433–1435.

BREWER, C. (1988) The management of opiate abuse: learning from other addictions. *Journal of Drug Issues*, **18**, 679–697.

CALLAHAN, C. M., GRANT, T. M., PHIPPS, P., *et al* (1992) Measurement of gestational cocaine exposure: sensitivity of infants' hair, meconium, and urine. *Journal of Pediatrics*, **120**, 763–768.

FRITCH, D., GROCE, Y. & RIEDERS, F. (1992) Cocaine and some of its products in hair by RIA and GC/MS. *Journal of Analytical Toxicology*, **16**, 112–114.

HARFORD, R. J. & KLEBER, H. D. (1978) Comparative validity of random-interval and fixed-interval urinalysis schedules. *Archives of General Psychiatry*, **35**, 356–359.

MAGURA, S., FREEMAN, R. C., SIDDIQI, Q., *et al* (1992) The validity of hair analysis for detecting cocaine and heroin use among addicts. *International Journal of the Addictions*, **27**, 51–69.

MIECZKOWSKI, T., LANDRESS, H. J., NEWEL, R., *et al* (1993) Testing hair for illicit drug use. *National Institute of Justice: Research in Brief* (NCJ 138539). Washington, DC: NIJ.

NAKAHARA, Y., TAKAHASHI, K., SHIMAMINE, M., *et al* (1991) Hair analysis for drug abuse: I. Determination of methamphetamine and amphetamine in hair by stable isotope dilution gas chromatography/mass spectrometry method. *Journal of Forensic Sciences*, **36**, 70–78.

Index

Compiled by STANLEY THORLEY